Columbia University
STUDIES IN ROMANCE PHILOLOGY AND
LITERATURE

LORENZO DA PONTE
Poet and Adventurer

COLUMBIA UNIVERSITY PRESS
SALES AGENTS

NEW YORK
LEMCKE & BUECHNER
30-32 EAST 20TH STREET

LONDON
HUMPHREY MILFORD
AMEN CORNER, E. C.

SHANGHAI
EDWARD EVANS & SONS, LTD.
30 NORTH SZECHUEN ROAD

LORENZO DA PONTE
FROM A HITHERTO UNPUBLISHED PORTRAIT, PAINTER UNKNOWN
AT COLUMBIA UNIVERSITY.

LORENZO DA PONTE

Poet and Adventurer

BY
JOSEPH LOUIS RUSSO, Ph.D.

New York
COLUMBIA UNIVERSITY PRESS
1922

All rights reserved

Copyright, 1922
BY COLUMBIA UNIVERSITY PRESS

Printed from type. Published May, 1922.

ALLA MEMORIA DI MIO PADRE
E
A MAMMUCCIA LONTANA

CONTENTS

CHAPTER	PAGE
INTRODUCTION	xi
I. YOUTH AND EARLY ADVENTURES	1
II. POET AND LIBERTINE	21
III. HOW DA PONTE BECAME A LIBRETTIST	41
IV. GLORY AND DOWNFALL	59
V. DA PONTE'S LONDON CAREER	83
VI. IN AMERICA	107
VII. LAST YEARS	125
APPENDIX—	
i. Letter to an Unknown Person in Sunbury, Pa.	141
ii. Letter from A. de Lamartine.	143
BIBLIOGRAPHY—	
i. The Principal Works of L. da Ponte	147
ii. Works about L. da Ponte	154
INDEX	159

ILLUSTRATIONS

      PAGE

LORENZO DA PONTE. From a hitherto unpublished portrait, painter unknown, at Columbia University . . . . *Frontispiece*

LORENZO DA PONTE. From a water-color in possession of Signor R. Rossi, in Vittorio Veneto 16

ANTONIO SALIERI. From an engraving by J. Neidl, after a portrait by Steinhauser von Treuberg, at the Hofbibliothek in Vienna 50

EMPEROR JOSEPH II OF AUSTRIA. From an old print . . 58

W. A. MOZART. From an engraving by Kohl after a medallion by Posch, at the Mozartmuseum in Salzburg . 62

FACSIMILE OF THE PROGRAM OF THE FIRST PERFORMANCE OF DON GIOVANNI 68

W. A. MOZART. From an unfinished portrait by J. Lange, at the Mozartmuseum in Salzburg 76

GIACOMO CASANOVA. From a portrait by Francesco Casanova, Dachoff Collection, Petrograd 84

LORENZO DA PONTE. From an old print 116

COLUMBIA COLLEGE AT THE TIME OF DA PONTE'S PROFESSORSHIP. Park Place, near Broadway, New York. "Drawn and Engraved expressly for the *New York Mirror*" 120

THE BEGINNING OF ITALIAN OPERA IN AMERICA. Facsimile of the announcement of the first performance of *Il Barbiere di Siviglia* in New York. From the *Evening Post* of November 29, 1825 126

MADAME MALIBRAN GARCIA. From an engraving by C. G. Child 128

FACSIMILE OF A LETTER BY LORENZO DA PONTE, DATED NOVEMBER, 7, 1824 142

"The man to whom credit is due for being the first in America to direct attention to the beauties of Italian literature, and expound Dante to an American audience, is Lorenzo Da Ponte."
Theodore W. Koch.

INTRODUCTION

Undoubtedly the greatest claim Lorenzo Da Ponte has to lasting remembrance is his connection with Mozart. To him belongs a share, modest though it be, in the glory of having enriched the world patrimony of art with such immortal treasures as *Le nozze di Figaro, Don Giovanni* and *Così fan tutte*.

But not only was he a librettist, and one of unusual skill and inspiration in a period in which the hopeless mediocrity of talent displayed by those engaged in that calling brought the very word "librettist" into disrepute,—he was also a writer of uncommon ability, a successful teacher, and one of the foremost pioneers of Italian culture in the United States.

By a curious coincidence 1825 marks the date at which the first two chairs of Italian were established, at Harvard and Columbia respectively, with Pietro Bachi and Lorenzo Da Ponte as professors. While, however, the former was a relatively obscure man and had only recently arrived in the United States, the appointment of Da Ponte crowned a teaching career of nearly twenty years, during which no less than two thousand American students had learned from him the beauties of the Italian language and acquired a first-hand appreciation of its world-famous authors, from Dante and Petrarch down to that young legion of writers and poets with whom the movement of the Risorgimento had its inception.

For a period of over thirty years—the last years of

his adventurous existence—Da Ponte lived in the United States, for the most part in New York City. Seldom if ever indeed had a man of a more interesting personality come to these shores from Europe. In the course of his long life, the term of which embraced the birth and death of Byron, Scott, Foscolo, Monti, Leopardi, Mozart, Beethoven and Napoleon, he had been by turns priest, poet and professor of rhetoric in Italy; poet to the Imperial Theatre and gallant abbé in Austria; librettist and bookseller in England; in America, tradesman, distiller, poet, man of letters, teacher, bookseller and impresario. He it was who, dreaming of founding a permanent seat for Italian opera in America, and to this dream devoting all his enthusiasm and unbounded energy as well as the feeble resources of his purse, opened the first Italian Opera House in the United States.

Of so eventful a career he himself has given his own account in his *Memorie,* a work which, curiously enough, has been translated into French and German, but never into English.[1] The book, well written and full of interest for the vivid picture it gives of the persons with whom the poet came in contact, as well as of the places where he lived and of the romantic period in which the earlier part of his existence was spent, has only a single fault: its truthfulness cannot be relied upon. When facts are against him, Da Ponte either omits them or, often enough, deliberately distorts them to suit his own purposes. This state of the case had been suspected for some time, but only recently have investigations, made by certain Italian

---

[1] While this work is going to press I learn that an English translation of the *Memorie* is being prepared by Mr. Walter Littlefield of New York.

scholars, and the publication of documentary evidence, rendered the matter certain.

It has been my object in writing this book to present a new detailed story of the life of Lorenzo Da Ponte, utilizing all the available material and combining therewith the results of my own research.

The sources of which I have made use are: (1) the *Memorie*, (2) other works by Da Ponte, (3) letters written to, by or about him, (4) biographical essays dealing with his career, (5) books concerning persons more or less directly connected with his life. Having been able to secure all the existing editions of the *Memorie*, I have selected, as the basis for references and citations in this work, the edition which I have found to be the most accurate, viz. that published by G. Gambarin and F. Nicolini (Bari, Giuseppe Laterza & Figli, 1918). Da Ponte's own narrative has been followed step by step, and his version accepted whenever there was no strong evidence against its veracity.

Those of his other works which have been of use in clearing up doubtful points are, primarily, his poems (especially his *Stanze al patrizio Pietro Zaguri*), a *Compendium* of his life, which he wrote years before the *Memorie*, and the pamphlets published by him in connection with his New York operatic ventures.

As for his personal letters, a considerable number of them had already been published by Jacopo Bernardi as long ago as 1871, in his work entitled *Memorie compendiate di Lorenzo Da Ponte*, and of these good use has been made by Angelo Marchesan, the most important of Da Ponte's biographers.

In addition, Pompeo Molmenti's recent publication of Giacomo Casanova's correspondence (*Carteggi*

Casanoviani, Palermo, R. Sandron, 1917), has brought to light several letters written by our Poet to the famous Venetian adventurer, as well as many letters of Zaguri and others, dealing with events of Da Ponte's life. Thus much has been learned of Da Ponte's activities which was not recorded in his autobiography. This material has been of invaluable assistance in the production of the present work.

Here it may be mentioned that I have had the good fortune of finding, in the Manuscript Department of the New York Public Library, a letter written by Da Ponte in 1824 which sheds new light on a phase of his life in America. This letter, accompanied by an English translation, is reproduced in the appendix.

Numerous writers have had their say on Da Ponte —some of them shortly after his death, and theirs is a valuable contribution inasmuch as it comes from men personally acquainted with the Poet; others have written quite recently, but, except for Marchesan, few have attempted to give a complete survey of Da Ponte's life, some having limited themselves to a particular period of his career, while most of the writers have only published short magazine articles, not infrequently full of inaccuracies.

Marchesan's book (Treviso, Tipografia Turazza, 1900) is a brilliant piece of composition covering all the material available at the time of writing and giving a detailed analysis of the Poet's literary productivity. It has, besides, the merit of presenting a number of poems not before published, prominent among which are those composed by Da Ponte during his professorship in the Seminary of Treviso. An exception that might be taken to the tone of this important monograph, is that Marchesan, while showing great severity towards Da Ponte's religious backslidings—a natural attitude since the author is a Catholic priest—is far too lenient towards the other shortcomings of the Poet. This, added to the fact that many obscure points of Da Ponte's life have been cleared up only recently, since the completion of Marchesan's book, and not in a way to enhance his reputation, has the effect of making Marchesan's picture of the man's personality seem all too flattering.

Other Italian writers who have turned their attention to Da Ponte's life, are, to mention only a few: Montani (who in 1828 wrote a few articles in the *Antologia* of Florence), Bartolomeo Gamba, Emilio De Marchi, Attilio Centelli, Domenico Giurati, Cesare Lozzi,—all of whom treated the subject in short sketches; and, in recent years, F. Novati, who made casual reference to Da Ponte in connection with Mozart; Serafino Paggi, author of a preface to the Martini edition of the *Memorie,* in which comparison is made of our Poet's autobiography with that of Goldoni; Pompeo Molmenti (already mentioned), who in his *Carteggi Casanoviani* introduces Da Ponte's letters with a short summary of his career; Aldo Ravà, who published some of our Poet's unedited works; and finally Fausto Nicolini, author of very scholarly and illuminating notes to his edition of the *Memorie.* To the last mentioned I am particularly indebted.

In France, in addition to M. C. D. de la Chevanne, who offered in abridged form a translation of the *Memorie,* the only writer who, to my knowledge, has treated the subject, is no less a personage than Lamartine. His article in the *Cours familier de Littérature* (vol. v, p. 406, *et seq.*), reproduced by La Chevanne as an introduction to his own work, deserves mention for the sheer beauty of its brilliant style and the fame of its author.

More accurate studies were made by Germans, of whom I shall mention here Alfred Meissner, Markus Landau and E. von Löhner. The last mentioned published, in 1884, a series of articles in the *Wiener Zeitung,* in which important results of his own investigations were brought out.

Much interesting material on Da Ponte's life in New York was contributed by American writers. The first and perhaps the most important contribution is that of Samuel Ward. His *Sketch on the Life of Lorenzo Da Ponte,* first published in the *New York Mirror* of August 1838 (the month in which the Poet died), and republished some years later in pamphlet form, gives a short account of Da Ponte's life as it had been made known through the *Memorie,* and is particularly interesting for the details it contains of the Poet's death and funeral. Nearly all subsequent articles on Da Ponte which have appeared in the United States are based mainly on this little work.

Dr. John W. Francis, a prominent New York physician, who attended Da Ponte in his last illness, also wrote about him, without however telling anything new, in his book entitled *Old New York,* the first edition of which dates from 1866.

The next to deal with Da Ponte's life was Henry T. Tuckerman, who in 1868 published an article on the subject in *Putnam's Magazine.* His sketch, vividly written, but replete with inaccuracies, offers very pleasant reading, and is not without importance, as this writer also was personally acquainted with the Poet.

An original study of sources emanates from the

gifted pen of Henry E. Krehbiel, to-day dean of the musical critics of New York. His article "Da Ponte in New York," which first appeared in the *New York Tribune* of August 28th, 1887, and was later included in his *Music and Manners in the Classical Period,* is especially noteworthy. In it the story of Da Ponte's professorship in Columbia University is for the first time reinforced by documentary evidence, and the vain efforts of the writer to trace the ultimate fate of the remains of the old Poet are set forth in a conclusive manner.

Among other contributions of a certain importance were that of the late Prof. George R. Carpenter of Columbia University, who published an article on Da Ponte in the *Columbia Literary Monthly* (April 1895), and that of the distinguished Dante scholar, Theodore W. Koch, who, in a study which appeared in the *Fifteenth Annual Report of the Dante Society* (1896), dwelt on his merits as a pioneer exponent in the United States of the Italian literature, and of Dante in particular.

Works which have been helpful, either because I have derived from them information on some special phase of Da Ponte's life or because they had a bearing on the times and places in which he lived, are: Casanova's *Mémoires;* that magnificent work on Venice, *Venice, its Individual Growth, etc.,* by Molmenti; several biographies of Mozart, of which I shall mention here only those by Jahn and Nohl; *Mozart's Operas* by Edward J. Dent; Arturo Farinelli's article on *Don Giovanni* in the *Giornale storico della letteratura italiana* (Turin, 1896); Michael Kelly's *Reminiscences;* Robert Eitner's *Biographisch-bibliographisches Quellen-Lexikon der Musiker und Musikgelehrten; Life and*

Letters of Fitz-Greene Halleck by James Grant Wilson,—and others of minor importance.

To all the foregoing writers I gratefully acknowledge my indebtedness, and I take this occasion to express my thanks also to Dr. Arthur Livingston, who first directed my attention to this subject, to President Nicholas Murray Butler of Columbia University, from whom I received the warmest encouragement through Prof. John L. Gerig, and to the latter, to Professors Raymond Weeks and Dino Bigongiari, and to my friend, Mr. Charles Huguenin, each of whom furnished me with most helpful advice.

What I owe to Professor Henry Alfred Todd can hardly be adequately expressed. From the first stages of my work to the very last he has been my guide, mentor and critic, and whatever merit this book may possess I ascribe unhesitatingly to his inspiring influence.

Finally I wish to mention my deep appreciation to my wife, who, with never-failing patience, has assisted me in collecting the large amount of material utilized, and whose criticism has often been of much value to me.

Meadville, Pa., March 20th, 1922.

LORENZO DA PONTE
Poet and Adventurer

CHAPTER I

Youth and Early Adventures

The name Da Ponte appears more than once, and not without glory, in the history of the Republic of Venice. Besides a Doge, Nicolò (1492?-1585) who represented the *Serenissima*, along with the Patriarch, at the Ecumenical Council of Trent, we find three *Procuratori di San Marco* by the same name; several senators, ambassadors, and prelates; in the field of arts, an architect, Giovanni Antonio Da Ponte (1512-97), who built the famous Rialto Bridge across the Grand Canal; and no less than five noted painters: —Jacopo Da Ponte (1510-92), and his four sons, Francesco (1548-91), Giambattista (1553-1613), Leandro (1558-1623), and Girolamo (1560-1622), all of these better known as the Bassanos from the town of their birth.

Not of so distinguished a family, however, was Lorenzo Da Ponte. He was born of Jewish parents, on March 10th, 1749, in the Ghetto of Ceneda[1]; his

---

[1] This town, now called Vittorio Veneto, in the province of Treviso, is the same which gave the name to the final victory of the Italian armies over the Austrians in the World War (Oct. 24-Nov. 3, 1918).

father, a leather dealer, was Geremia Conegliano, his mother was "Ghella" (Rachel) Pincherle, and he himself bore the given name of Emanuele.[2]

His mother died when he was five years old, leaving him with two younger brothers, Baruch (born April 9th, 1752) and Anania (born April 1st, 1754). Nine years later, through the efforts of Monsignor Lorenzo Da Ponte, Bishop of Ceneda, which town still cherishes a remembrance of this bishop's noble character and pious zeal,[3] Geremia Conegliano was persuaded to embrace Christianity together with his children. The ceremony of baptism took place with extraordinary pomp in the cathedral on August 29th, 1763, as shown by the church records, and the Bishop not only administered the baptism himself, but, following an established custom, gave his name to the neophytes. Thus Geremia, Emanuele, Baruch and Anania Conegliano became respectively Gaspare, Lorenzo, Girolamo and Luigi Da Ponte.

The underlying motive, however, which actuated Geremia's conversion was probably the fact that he had arranged a marriage with a Catholic maiden, Orsola Pasqua Paietta; for it appears from the church records that he was wedded to her only twelve days after he had been received into the Catholic faith. He was then over forty-one years of age, while his bride was but seventeen.

---

[2] The only allusion to his origin which can be found in the *Memorie* is his assertion of an early knowledge of Hebrew. But he is more explicit in his stanzas to Pietro Zaguri, published for the first time in Vienna in 1788, in which he attributes to his enemies the following invective: "Let us throw him back into the Ghetto, whence came his despicable ancestors!"

[3] Attilio Centelli, *Gli avventurieri della letteratura, Lorenzo Da Ponte*, in *Natura ed Arte* (Milan, Anno II, 1893, No. 21, Oct. 1st.).

It is quite evident that Lorenzo did not find the prospect of having a stepmother altogether pleasing. Moreover, he had long desired an education; for, hitherto, his father had done very little for him in this regard. True it is that at the age of eleven he had had a tutor, but the man proved inefficient and brutal, and was dismissed when his character was revealed to the father. The boy, left at that time solely to his own devices, had eagerly read the few books he had found among the rubbish in the attic of his home,—worthless books for the most part, except for a few volumes of Metastasio's dramas, which certainly must have created a deep impression on his precocious mind.

He determined now to seek aid from the Bishop, who, assuming all the expense, willingly assisted him and also his brother Girolamo to enter the Seminary of Ceneda.

At that time Latin was the principal subject in such schools, and within two years Lorenzo and his brother had made enough progress to enable them to write "with some degree of elegance" in that language. Other subjects, even Italian, were neglected, and our Poet admits that he could not have written then a few lines in his native tongue without many errors. This was the type of education imparted to youths destined for the priesthood, and, as Lorenzo says, his father, "guided more by his circumstances than his paternal duty," desired him to become a priest, "although such a career," the Poet adds, "was absolutely contrary to my inclination and character."[4]

Fortunately among his teachers there was a young professor, the Abbé Cagliari, recently graduated from

---

[4] *Memorie*, Edition Gambarin e Nicolini (Bari, Laterza, 1918), vol. i, p. 6.

the University of Padua and an enthusiastic expounder of Italian literature, who awakened in his most gifted students a love for the Italian classics. Encouraged by him and stimulated by the example of Girolamo Perucchini and Michele Colombo,[5] two of his school-fellows for whom he preserved a warm friendship throughout his life, Lorenzo devoted himself to the study of the Italian poets with feverish assiduity. In less than six months he had committed to memory almost the whole *Inferno,* the best sonnets of Petrarch and the most beautiful passages of Ariosto and Tasso, while at the same time trying his own Muse in competition with his two friends.

With Colombo he had also another kind of rivalry, since the two seminarists were both in love with a fascinating girl of Ceneda. Her name, not mentioned in the *Memorie,* is revealed in a letter written, in his old age, by Da Ponte to his life-long friend: she was a certain Pierina Raccanelli.[6]

That the rivalry between the two boys was not always friendly, appears from the following anecdote related by A. Pezzana, author of a *Life of Colombo* (based mainly on autobiographical notes) which he

[5] Michele Colombo (1747-1838) was also a native of Ceneda. He acquired a certain reputation in the field of letters, wrote a book of verses and a linguistic treatise: *Lezioni sopra le doti di una colta favella.*

[6] The letter, dated from New York, August 4th, 1828, contains this passage: "I remember the sonnets made by us in turn for our rector: *Quanto è possente amor,* and the other: *Candido, leggiadruccio cagnoletto;* and the two verses which you made for Father Quietevvè: *Qual picciol mosca ad affamato lupo, Tal mezzo od un sol pane A questa fera immane,* and even the first sonnet you wrote for me when I was in love (sixty-five years ago) with Pierina Raccanelli, which begins: *Del picciol Meschio in sulla riva amena.*" Jacopo Bernardi, *Memorie di Lorenzo Da Ponte, etc.* (Florence, Le Monnier, 1871), p. 186.

wrote for the collection of biographies edited by E. De Tipaldo:

"Colombo, easily aroused to anger but also quick to recognize his fault, dashed one day from Da Ponte's room while the latter was in bed, and, returning soon after armed with a long knife, rushed forward to throw himself against his friend. Lorenzo, who promptly saw his danger, jumped from the bed, grasped one of the iron bed-slats and put himself on guard. This brought Colombo to his senses; he threw the knife to the floor, Da Ponte did the same with his improvised weapon, both burst into laughter and embraced each other, each begging the other's pardon."[7]

Neither did they spare a certain amount of trouble to the Fathers of the Seminary. In reminiscence of his youthful days, the almost octogenarian Colombo wrote to Daniele Francesconi, librarian of the University of Padua:

"Da Ponte was my school-fellow in the Seminary of Ceneda. Never was a friend dearer to me; he belonged to me and I to him, two crazy heads of the first rank. Nobody could believe the wild things we did in that place; we were both expelled and then readmitted, for, crazy as we were, we were even so better than others who were wiser than we."[8]

Notwithstanding all his faults, Lorenzo's love for study must have been sincere, if, as he tells us, he went even so far as to steal a few hides from his father's shop, in order to barter them for books.[9] But a serious illness,—which for six months endangered his life,—family reverses, and the death of his benefactor the Bishop, took him away from the Seminary for

---

[7] E. De Tipaldo, *Biografia degli Italiani illustri*, vol. vi. p. 107.
[8] Bernardi, *L. Da Ponte*, p. 180.
[9] *Memorie*, vol. i, pp. 10-11.

over a year. Through these unfortunate circumstances he was compelled to renounce the hand of a "noble and beautiful" girl[10] whom he loved ardently (probably the already mentioned Pierina Raccanelli), and to decide in favor of the career which so little suited his nature.

It was Canon Ziborghi of the Cathedral of Ceneda, who, anxious to realize the hopes which the late Mgr. Da Ponte had placed in him and his two brothers, came to their assistance and put all three in the Seminary of Portogruaro, so that they might complete their education and eventually enter the priesthood. There —he was now twenty years old—young Da Ponte spent his first year studying philosophy and mathematics, while not neglecting poetry. He was well liked and highly appreciated by his superiors, who even appointed him a tutor at the end of the school-year. From a letter written to his friend Colombo[11] we learn also that, at the same time, he had been admitted to the major orders. The step was taken which for many years was going to be the primary cause of his many difficulties and sorrows.

In January 1771, he and his brothers spent ten days in Venice to recover from malaria. The impression produced on him by the gay life of that bewitching city must have haunted him on his return to the Seminary, and the letters he sends now to Colombo reflect this disturbed state of mind. "I am thankful to you," he writes, "for often mentioning me to our common friends, of whom I think only four are left. I would consider myself fortunate if I could count as many in this Seminary! Many indeed are

---

[10] *Memorie*, vol. i, p. 11.
[11] Bernardi, *L. Da Ponte*, p. 149.

attached to me, but it is not the sort of attachment for which I am longing."[12] It will soon be seen where this restlessness carried him.

A song in honor of St. Louis, composed and recited by him at the end of his second year in the Seminary, so much pleased the Bishop, Mgr. Gabrielli, that the latter appointed him to the chair of rhetoric. It seems that Lorenzo hesitated before accepting, since he was anxious to perfect himself in Hebrew, a language he says he had "intensively studied" in his childhood, and to familiarize himself with the Greek poets, the knowledge of whom he thought a necessary accomplishment for a good poet. Finally he accepted, and, to quote his own words: "at an age in which I myself needed to learn no end of things, I took up the arduous task of teaching literature to others."[13]

During the following summer vacation, without any doubt, he was in Venice again (a fact not mentioned in his *Memorie,* nor by any of his biographers), for, as will presently appear, his love affair with the Venetian noblewoman Angela Tiepolo dates back to that time. Of her and her weighty influence on Da Ponte's life there will be occasion later to speak at length.

At the reopening of the schools the next autumn, we find our Poet back in the Seminary in his new capacity. His lectures and the method of his teaching acquired for him considerable popularity among the students, but this very brilliancy aroused criticism on the part of his colleagues, who taunted him with being a poetaster devoid of any learned foundation. The situation, as will easily be understood, grew even

[12] Bernardi, *L. Da Ponte,* p. 152.
[13] *Memorie,* vol. i, pp. 12-13.

worse when, on April 14th, 1772, he was chosen by the Bishop to take the place of the vice-rector, recently deceased.

Announcing the news of this to his friend Colombo, in a letter dated the 23d of the same month, Lorenzo wrote:

"My new position as vice-rector, besides giving me a distinguished place in the faculty, yields me forty ducats yearly. My duties consist in supervising discipline, giving the address at the beginning of the school year, conducting the final public *accademia,* and teaching Italian to fifty-two of the best students of this Seminary."[14]

The public *accademia* to which he alludes was quite an important institution in the schools of that period. At the end of every school-year the professor of rhetoric, as a duty inherent in his office, had to write several compositions in Latin, Italian and Greek on a subject of his own choice, compositions which, distributed to the best students, were recited by them publicly on the day of the *conclusione degli studi,* as it was called (our commencement), at which, in addition to the students, were convened the Bishop, the Monsignori of the cathedral, the town magistrates, and other prominent guests.[15] It may be added that the above mentioned compositions were as a rule in poetical form, and that the subject was treated *pro et contra,* so that the proceeding was more or less of a debate.

Da Ponte seized this opportunity to refute the criticisms of his enemies, by composing a number of

[14] Bernardi, *L. Da Ponte,* p. 166.
[15] Angelo Marchesan, *Della Vita e delle Opere di Lorenzo Da Ponte* (Treviso, Tip. Turazza, 1900), pp. 52-53.

YOUTH AND EARLY ADVENTURES

Italian and Latin poems treating natural phenomena, one of which, dealing with odors, in the form of a dithyramb in the style of Redi, was highly praised.[16]

Originality could certainly not be claimed for these verses even by a lenient critic; the element of imitation is too evident. They show, however, considerable purity of language and a promising facility.

In a letter written to Colombo,[17] March 27th, 1773 is recorded as the date on which he celebrated mass for the first time. That was also his last year as a professor in the Seminary of Portogruaro, for, having become embittered by the persistent antagonism of which he believed himself a victim[18] and not being able, we may surmise, to endure longer the separation from Angela Tiepolo, he resigned at the close of the school year and went to Venice.[19]

The Queen of the Adriatic, deprived through fatal historical circumstances of all the elements which had gained for her in past centuries such a glorious leadership among European powers, had become at that time the Sybaris of the modern world. A morbid craving for pleasures had superseded all ancient virtues. From the noblest patrician to the lowest gondolier every one seemed pervaded by it, and, in addition, even more than to Paris, thousands of strangers

---

[16] The *Ditirambo sopra gli odori* was later published in the *Saggi Poetici dell' abate L. D. P., Poeta al servizio di S. M. cesarea* (Vienna, Imperial stamperia dei sordi e muti, 1788), in two volumes.

[17] Bernardi, *L. Da Ponte*, p. 172.

[18] The reader will soon discover that Da Ponte had a tendency to suspect envy and persecution everywhere.

[19] One of his "rivals" in Portogruaro was a priest of Ceneda against whom he later published anonymously in Venice a poem, mentioned by him in a letter to Colombo, which bears the date of June 27th, 1773 (Bernardi, *L. Da Ponte*, pp. 174-5).

from every part of Europe flocked there at all seasons of the year, to mingle in a continuous revel.

The general use of masks afforded a screen for unbridled license, a shield against public scandal; and even priests and nuns, thus protected by an *incognito* considered inviolable by general consent, indulged in the worldly pleasures they had vowed to renounce.[20] Year after year there occurred an unbroken succession of serenades, balls, sumptuous banquets, impressive ceremonies, for which occasions were eagerly sought whenever a new doge was inaugurated, a *procuratore* elected, or a foreign ambassador received. A Venetian contemporary of Da Ponte, famous for his adventurous life and therefore speaking from experience, gives us this bit of information:

"Les personnes de la bonne compagnie qui vont se promener à l' Erberia d' un peu bon matin sont convenues de dire que c' est pour jouir du plaisir de voir arriver des centaines de barques chargées de légumes, de fruits et de fleurs, qui viennent des nombreuses îles qui avoisinent la ville; mais tout le monde sait qu'il n'y a que les jeunes gens et les jeunes femmes qui ont passé la nuit dans les plaisirs de Cythère, dans les excès de la table, ou qui, désespérés par la fortune et victimes de l' imprudence, ont perdu leur dernier espoir au jeu, qui

---

[20] Pompeo Molmenti, in his *Venice, its Individual Growth from the Earliest Beginnings to the Fall of the Republic*, transl. by Horatio F. Brown (Chicago, McClurg, 1908), Part III, vol. ii, pp. 80-81, asserts that "an anonymous libel, published in Rome at the time of the Interdict of Paul V, declares that at Venice, 'some of the nuns have lovers who frequently visit and converse with them; that the lay sisters act as go-betweens; that during Carnival many nuns put on the mask, and their lovers come with their gondolas to take them out; or they go through the city on foot to entertainments, whence they return when they please.'" He quotes also Businello's lines:

> La monaca ch' a Dio xe consecrada
> Xe ogni dì alla finestra co l' amante.

aillent dans cet endroit pour respirer un air plus libre et calmer leur agitation."[21]

Gambling, in fact, tolerated by the government notwithstanding some occasional prohibitions, was indulged in on so great a scale that entire patrimonies were swept away. In the gorgeous rooms of the *Ridotto* throngs of masked gamblers crowded around tables at each of which presided some nobleman unmasked, in robe and wig; for the privilege of conducting the bank was reserved to that class alone; and—what made their degradation the more base—the nefarious business was carried on, as a rule, not with their own money but with that of some wealthy Jew. Worse still, even children were inducted into the use of playing cards, since from the age of four they were taught to read from decks bearing printed on each card the letters of the alphabet.[22] Gallantry, introduced from Spain a century before, had degenerated into that *cicisbeismo*, so vividly pictured by Goldoni in his plays,[23] which found recognition even in some marriage contracts, in which it was stipulated how many *cicisbei* the bride should be permitted to have and who they

[21] Giacomo Casanova, *Mémoires*, vol. iii, p. 184.
[22] Molmenti, *Venice*, Part III, vol. ii, p. 55.
[23] Pantalone, in scene xiv of the second act of *Le donne puntigliose*, exclaims:
"There are things which make one die of laughter, in a society where there are ladies with their *cavalieri serventi*. The ladies, stiff as statues, allow themselves to be adored. And the men,—one sighs here, another kneels there; one offers a cup, another picks a handkerchief from the floor; this one kisses a hand, that one offers his arm; one acts as a secretary, again another as a waiter, while the rest perfume, besprinkle, pet and flatter them. And the ladies whisper to each other, act in harmony and put the men under their feet: the sex triumphs, and men reduce themselves to the condition of slaves in chains, idolaters of beauty, profaners of their self-respect, and a scandal to youth."

were to be.[24] Often, however, the *cicisbeo's* place was usurped by one of those foppish little abbés, all made up, perfumed and powdered, who, despite the tonsure, danced the minuet, improvised madrigals and toasts, and excelled in all society graces.

Such was the whirlpool into which Lorenzo Da Ponte plunged after leaving the Seminary of Portogruaro. No wonder that, with his impulsive temperament, poetical nature and unusually attractive appearance, the young abbé was soon engulfed in all kinds of intrigues and adventures.[25]

To begin with, he found there Angela Tiepolo, for whom he admits having felt a very ardent passion. She was an extremely fascinating but at the same time most unscrupulous and capricious woman, belonging to one of those illustrious patrician families, so common at that time, which unrestrained profligacy had brought to almost absolute indigence.[26] Our poet, recalling in his old age this stormy period of his life, thus describes her:

"She was tiny, delicate, gentle; white as the snow, with soft and languishing eyes and two charming dimples in her cheeks, fresh as roses. She could not boast much

---

[24] Moroni, *I Minuetti* (Rome, 1880), p. 86.

[25] "Essendo nel bollor dell' età, di temperamento vivace e, al dire di tutti, avvenente della persona, mi lasciai trasportare dagli usi, dal comodo e dall' esempio alle voluttà ed ai divertimenti, dimenticando o negligendo quasi del tutto la letteratura e lo studio." *Memorie*, vol. i, p. 14.

[26] The family Tiepolo—"Teupolo" in the old spelling—belonged to the *Apostolic* order of nobility, and claimed Roman origin. Bartoldo Teupolo, the head of the family in 697, was one of the electors of the first Venetian Doge, Paolo Lucio Anafesto. In 1204, after the fall of Constantinople, when so many Venetian nobles were given titles of sovereignty over Greek islands, Giacomo Tiepolo was named Duke of Candia. The family gave two doges to the Republic, the above mentioned Giacomo and his son, Lorenzo.

mental culture, but she was gifted with such charm of manner and such witty conversation that she not only won her way into all hearts but captivated every one."[27]

In his autobiography Lorenzo informs us that his liaison with Angela Tiepolo lasted three years. "I do not believe," he writes, "that, during the three years which that liaison lasted, I learned anything which I did not know before or which was worth knowing."[28] And the assertion, which there is no reason to doubt, is repeated when he relates how the affair ended: "She who for three continuous years had kept me tied to her and whom I, even though far away, still loved ardently, gave herself to a new lover a few days after my departure."[29]

A number of his biographers, misinterpreting these passages, have assumed that the Poet's stay in Venice extended for three years.[30] The fact is, however, that Da Ponte remained there only one year, as appears from the official records of Lorenzo's departure from the Seminary of Portogruaro and of his appointment, as we shall see, to a chair in the Seminary of Treviso, and, furthermore, from a letter written by him to Colombo on October 8th, 1774.[31]

But since the end of this love affair occurred on January 1st, 1775,[32] that is to say, only shortly after

---

[27] *Memorie*, vol. i, p. 22. See Molmenti, *Venice*, Part III, vol. ii, p. 121.

[28] "Non credo, in tre anni di tempo che durò quella tresca, d' aver imparata cosa che pria non sapessi o che fosse pur degna di sapersi." *Memorie*, vol. i, p. 14.

[29] "Colei, che per tre anni continui mi tenne avvinto e ch'io anche in lontananza seguitava ad amare ferventemente, si diede in braccio, pochi dì dopo la mia partenza, a novello amante." *Memorie*, vol. i, p. 39.

[30] Marchesan (*L. Da Ponte*, p. 25) does not fall into this error.

[31] Bernardi, *L. Da Ponte*, p. 176.

[32] *Memorie*, vol. i, p. 39.

the Poet had left the city of St. Mark, the only way of accounting for the three years is to assume that he had been in Venice and started his intrigue in the autumn of 1771. Not only that, but we must also infer that prior to his leaving Portogruaro he undoubtedly made frequent trips to Venice to see his lady love; otherwise his assertion would hardly have any meaning.

Why Da Ponte in his *Memorie* should have abstained from mentioning the facts as they are here related, is easily explained: reprehensible as it was for him, a priest, to have led so disorderly a life, it would have been worse still for his reputation had he openly admitted, in a book written primarily for the conventional New York world of a century ago, that he was already a slave to passion when he ascended the altar to say his first mass, and that, in contravention of his new dignity, he had unconcernedly persisted in his relations as a lover.

It would be curious also to know whether the criticism which we know existed against him in the Seminary of Portogruaro, was not at least partly due to those frequent mysterious absences which we have surmised as occurring during the last two years of his stay in that institution.

Once in Venice, his time, as he tells us and as we readily believe, was entirely consumed by this passion. Occasionally, however, he frequented the Caffé Menegazzo (also known as the *Caffé de' Letterati*) half-way down the Merceria, which in fact was the resort of the literary world. There probably he met Gaspare and Carlo Gozzi, Giuseppe and Daniele Farsetti, Marco Forcellini, Niccolò Tron, Sebastiano Crotta, Natale dalle Laste, Paolo Balbi and Biagio Schiso, all members of that *Accademia dei Granelleschi* which delighted in harassing the famous Goldoni.[33]

It was while he was spending one evening in that place that a fantastic adventure is supposed to have happened to him.[34] A gondolier appeared there, beckoned to him and led him to his gondola, where a mysterious young woman was waiting. Da Ponte, who had thought he was summoned to meet Angela, and the lady, who on her part was expecting to be joined by her lover, recognized their error only on greeting each other as their boat was already gliding through the dark canal. The lady tried at first to induce Da Ponte to withdraw, but our gallant abbé was reluctant to let the occasion slip for starting a new romance, and exerted all his arts to win the lady's favor. From this chance meeting the affair took quite a serious turn, for Da Ponte admits that he was about to elope with her, when one night, as in a real melodrama, she was spirited away by order of the *Inquisitori di Stato* and secreted in a religious retreat outside Venice.

From the story as related with all kinds of details in the Poet's autobiography, we are informed that the

---

[33] "The Academy of the *Granelleschi*, founded in Venice in 1747, endeavored to correct the exaggerated emphasis of style by recalling writers to the earlier Tuscan models. It was a reaction against the literary taste of the Seicento, but they rapidly degenerated into another defect of style, by substituting for the bombastic and flowery the nerveless and flaccid." Molmenti, *Venice*, Part III, vol. ii, pp. 166-7. See also: Carlo Gozzi, *Mem. int.* vol. i, p. 245 *et seq.*; and Farsetti, *Mem. dell' Accademia Granellesca*, Treviso, Trento, 1799. Gaspare Gozzi (1713-86) and his brother Carlo (1722-1806) occupy an important position in the Italian literature of the XVIII century; the latter was also a reputable dramatist. Giuseppe Farsetti (1720-92) wrote elegantly in prose and verse.

[34] *Memorie*, vol. i, pp. 14-24.

young woman was no less than the daughter of a Neapolitan duke and that she had fled from her home to escape the persecution of her stepmother.

Romantic as all this may seem, another adventure which sounds like an Arabian Nights tale is told, with the same abundance of details, in the *Memorie*.[35] An eccentric old man, who had accumulated a considerable fortune by begging on the Rialto bridge, having noticed Da Ponte's generosity and charitable disposition, invited him to come to his home. There, after having told him the story of his life, he proposed to him point-blank that he marry his only daughter, a beautiful girl just out of the convent, offering at the same time half of his treasure as her dowry. Charmed by the girl's attractive and innocent appearance as, in response to her father's summons, she entered the room, and momentarily tempted by the sight of piles of shining gold in an open chest, our Lorenzo was inclined to close the bargain, when the recollection of his Angela prompted him nobly to refuse. The rest of the evening, however, he spent with the old man and his fair daughter, and returned only late at night to the Tiepolo home, in which he was living. There he was confronted by Angela in a furiously jealous tantrum, for as soon as he approached her room, she, without speaking a word, hurled an ink bottle at him. His hand, with which he had instinctively protected his face, was quite severely wounded by the impact of the broken glass, and it was only at the sight of his blood that her anger subsided. But the following morning he was amazed on awakening to discover that his hair, which he was accustomed to wear shoulder length as was the fash-

---

[35] *Memorie*, vol. i, pp. 27-34.

LORENZO DA PONTE
FROM A WATER-COLOR IN POSSESSION OF SIGNOR R. ROSSI,
IN VITTORIO VENETO.

ion, had been most dexterously but unbecomingly clipped during the night by this modern Delilah. Her purpose had been to prevent him from leaving the house, and he was obliged, *bon gré mal gré,* to yield to her caprice. This cost him dear: a noble Venetian lady whose two sons he had been tutoring, and by whom he had been liberally paid, came personally to inquire into the cause of his non-appearance, and, finding him in such a dishevelled state and among such dissipated people, promptly dismissed him.

In a letter written to Colombo on January 19th, 1774,[36] he relates his misfortune to his old friend, informing him, however, that a new position has been offered him which he can secure by paying a commission of ten sequins[37] to an agent. Of course, Colombo is asked to send the money, for Da Ponte is penniless and nobody is willing to help him. "Remember," he says, "that any hesitation on your part would be the same as to deny me help, and this would mean my ruin."

But this letter, showing that his dismissal as a tutor occurred before January 19th, contradicts the assertion made in the Poet's autobiography that his visit to the old beggar took place on the first Sunday in Lent and was the result of generous alms he had given to the man on the morning of Ash Wednesday. Naturally, this renders us all the more skeptical as to the veracity of the tale. And not only so; is not the suspicion somewhat warranted that the new position, referred to in the letter but not even vaguely men-

---

[36] Bernardi, *L. Da Ponte,* p. 176.
[37] A gold coin first issued by the Venetian republic in the thirteenth century and known afterwards all over Europe. Its value was about $2.25 in United States gold.

tioned in the *Memorie,* was only a plea to induce Colombo to loosen his purse-strings?

That Lorenzo's situation was decidedly unenviable may readily be believed. Without means of honorable self-support, worn out by his dissipated life, unable to devote any time to work or study, he saw no way out of his troubles. Nor was this all, for he had much to endure that was unpleasant from Angela's brother, a corrupted youth and an inveterate gambler, who induced his sister and her lover to follow him night after night to the *Ridotto* or to other gambling places. Da Ponte's only means of maintaining harmony with him was to furnish him with money whenever he had any; and in order to compel Da Ponte to disgorge young Tiepolo was not at all scrupulous as to the method employed, even going so far, on at least one occasion, as to threaten the abbé *armata manu.*[38]

What brought this miserable state of affairs to an end was probably the strong influence persistently exerted on weak-willed Lorenzo by his brother Girolamo, a priest also, but of a much more serious nature and of an entirely different character, who at that time was a tutor in a distinguished Venetian family.

Da Ponte mentions at this point of his autobiography a peculiar incident which is supposed to have influenced him to accept his brother's advice to leave the dangerous city at once: a priest, who had been accounted a friend of his, after having dined with him stole his cape, pawned it and gambled with the ill-gotten money, losing it all. The shock of seeing to what depths of depravity vice could lead, awakened Da Ponte to his own peril. Disregarding Angela's

[38] *Memorie,* vol. i, p. 35.

prayers, tears and threats, he departed immediately for his home town.

Ten days later, according to the *Memorie,* he and his brother were engaged as professors in the Seminary of Treviso, and our Poet informs us that Girolamo's main reason for accepting the new position was in order to be near him.[39] This appointment, however, was not made as suddenly as we are told in his autobiography, for in a letter which he wrote to Colombo from Venice on October 8th, 1774,[40] he begged his friend to prevail upon a priest of Ceneda to retract the accusations he had made against his character to Mgr. Giustiniani, Bishop of Treviso, in view of which the latter had refused to give him a chair in his Seminary. Among the scandalous acts imputed to him was his having eloped with a woman of Ceneda,—"a thing," he adds, "which you well know I never even dreamed of doing."

It thus appears that, when he went to Ceneda, he had been planning already for some time to leave Venice, and that in going there he had a definite purpose in mind: to promote the success of his candidacy. The result was satisfactory, for the names of Lorenzo and Girolamo Da Ponte appear on the records of the Seminary of Treviso for the school-year 1774-75, the former as master of literature (*umanità*), the second as master of lower grammar.[41] But, although separated from Angela, our Poet did not completely sever

---

[39] *Memorie,* vol. i, p. 38.

[40] The letter has already been quoted as a proof that Lorenzo's stay in Venice did not last over a year. Bernardi, *L. Da Ponte,* p. 176.

[41] Marchesan (*L. Da Ponte,* p. 33) informs us from the records of the Seminary of Treviso, that, in addition to lodging and board, Lorenzo received a yearly salary of 217 Venetian *lire,* while his brother Girolamo was paid only 155 *lire.*

his relations with her until January 1st, 1775, if we may credit his extremely dramatic version of the end of the affair.[42] It seems that she used to write him endearing letters every day. On the above-mentioned date he received a short note from her urging him to hasten to Venice, if he cared at all for her honor and life. Da Ponte obeyed her summons, but when, very late at night, he reached the house where he was supposed to meet her, a man, whom he recognized by his voice as his old servant, approached him in the darkness and implored him not to enter, adding that he had overheard the discussion of a plot against him. That "perfidious woman" had written the note in question at the instigation of her new lover, a certain Dondorologi, who, being madly jealous of his predecessor, had demanded as a proof of her love that she lure Da Ponte into her house, where it was his plan to give him a severe beating. Moved by anger, jealousy and a desire for revenge, Lorenzo, ignoring the warning, dashed into the house. There he found Angela alone. One might naturally assume that this fact would have made him doubt the servant's story; but when Angela moved towards him to embrace him, he thrust her aside and, after a violent scene, left her forever. Only afterwards did he learn from the same old servant that his rival had actually been there up to within a few minutes of his arrival, and that, bored by waiting, he had just left to spend the rest of the night in gambling. At any rate, the affair came to an end, and on his return to Treviso, Da Ponte entered upon a period of study and intellectual activity.

[42] *Memorie*, vol. i, pp. 39-40.

CHAPTER II

Poet and Libertine

Altogether Da Ponte remained two years in the Seminary of Treviso. There—at any rate as far as we know—he led the sort of life that his calling demanded. The whole atmosphere was favorable to his studies; he enjoyed the esteem and protection of Mgr. Giustiniani, himself a scholar; he was in charge of the library, which under his supervision was considerably enlarged; and he had the satisfaction of seeing his classes frequented by youths of talent, eager to acquire from his eloquent lectures a true appreciation of literature.

Nor were learned and congenial friends lacking. Besides his brother Girolamo, described in the *Memorie*[1] as a man who combined high intellectual qualities with great integrity of character, wisdom and modesty, he had the privilege of associating closely with men of established reputation in the field of letters, such for example as Giulio Trento.[2] Probably it was the latter who introduced Lorenzo into the society of Treviso, which our Poet calls *brillante* and *amica delle lettere e de' letterati*,[3] and where

---

[1] Vol. i, p. 37.
[2] He was a writer of extensive learning and exquisite taste. His rather large production in prose and verse was highly praised in his time. Especially noteworthy is his translation of Sallust. See Angelo Marchesan's article on him, in *La Voce del Cuore*, Treviso, vol. viii, No. 15, August 1st, 1897.
[3] *Memorie*, vol. i, p. 41.

there is every reason to believe that, with his witty conversation and handsome appearance, he soon made himself popular.

His reputation as a poet and the esteem in which he was held by the Bishop and the learned circle of Treviso, were appreciably increased when he read in an *Accademia*[4] his poem *Il Cecchino o sia la storia del cane e del gatto,* a composition worthy of note and far superior to anything he had before written. This and other literary successes, coupled with his efficient method of teaching, won for him, at the conclusion of the first school-year, a promotion to the more important position of professor of rhetoric, while the chair he had previously occupied was assigned to his brother Girolamo.[5]

In his autobiography our Poet tells us that such a distinction was not obtained without arousing deep dissatisfaction on the part of colleagues of older standing. That this criticism had no foundation he states emphatically, claiming that his fellow-teachers, though men of sound learning and considerable experience, "were entirely devoid of that genius and good taste which are the first requisites of art and which, if not bestowed by nature, are rarely if ever acquired."[6]

---

[4] Marchesan (*L. Da Ponte*, p. 39) believes, and perhaps rightly so, that *Il Cecchino* was recited either in the *Accademia dei Solleciti* or in the *Colonia Arcadica* of Treviso. The poem was published for the first time in the *Saggi Poetici* (Vienna, 1788), reprinted in Treviso (1817) on the occasion of the wedding Farra Soligo-Boregan; again in Treviso (1819) by Giuseppe Monico; then by the author in the last volume of the second edition of his *Memorie*, and finally by Bernardi (*L. Da Ponte*, pp. 345-52).

[5] Marchesan (*L. Da Ponte*, p. 49) gives the information that in their new positions Lorenzo and Girolamo Da Ponte received respectively a yearly salary of 279 and 217 Venetian lire.

[6] *Memorie*, vol. i, p. 41.

He even goes so far as to assert that if good taste and a right method of studying Italian literature were introduced in the Seminary of Treviso, the credit is due to him and his brother,—an assertion flatly contradicted by Marchesan,[7] who, although not denying that the two Da Pontes may have had exceptional teaching ability, offers convincing proof that a high standard of instruction in Italian literature had always been maintained in that institution.

As has been seen, one of the most important duties of a professor of rhetoric was that of composing the poems to be recited at the *Accademia* held at the end of the school-year. That task in 1776 fell to Lorenzo, who selected as his theme the rather eccentric question whether men organized in society are happier than they would be if they had remained in a primitive state.[8] Nobody familiar with Rousseau's essay on the question raised by the *Académie de Dijon* in 1749:[9] *Si le progrès des sciences et des arts a contribué à corrompre ou épurer les moeurs,* or with his *Discours sur l'inégalité,* will fail to recognize the source from which our Poet derived his inspiration.

The new theories which had come from France, had for some time been the subject of lively discussions among the *beaux esprits* of Italy, and we can easily imagine how these theories must have appealed

---

[7] L. Da Ponte, pp. 49-52.

[8] The original text of the theme is: *Se gli uomini per le leggi e per le distribuzioni della civil società abbiano il sentiero della felicità umana appianato o ristretto, o se per queste leggi medesime sieno in rapporto alla loro felicità nel primiero stato rimasti.* The complete collection of poems composed by Da Ponte for this *Accademia* was published for the first time by Angelo Marchesan, in his frequently quoted work on our Poet, from a manuscript he found in the *Archivio Capitolare* of Treviso.

[9] Strange coincidence: Da Ponte's year of birth.

to the ardent temperament and unbridled fancy of Lorenzo, whose nature, after all, had remained unchanged, and who felt as keenly as ever the burden of duties contrary to his inclinations and the tyranny of the restrictions imposed upon him by the exigencies of society. The influence exerted on him by Rousseau seems to have lasted even up to his old age, for there are reasons for believing that he had often in mind Jean-Jacques' *Confessions* while writing his *Memorie*.[10]

The argument selected for the *Accademia* was treated by Da Ponte in four Latin and eleven Italian poems, preceded by a preface in Italian prose to be recited as a sort of introduction. An established custom required that the poems should be in Latin, Italian, and sometimes Greek, and that both to demonstrate the poet's skill and to give a certain variety to the whole affair, different meters should be employed. Lorenzo strictly adhered to this tradition and his fifteen compositions—of which, in order not to exhaust the reader's patience, only the first five will be briefly commented upon—differ from one another not only in style and rhythm, but in conception as well, each poem having a separate theme.

Man, he says in his preface, longs for happiness, but perfect happiness, involving total and secure possession of the *summum bonum,* is unattainable, and therefore all that he can hope to reach on this earth is an approximate happiness, that is, one approaching

---

[10] In addition to the similarity of character of the two books, there are many points in the *Memorie* which strikingly recall the *Confessions*. Like the French writer, Lorenzo also boasts a crude sincerity, which however hardly bears a serious investigation; both men confess themselves guilty of petty thefts in their youth, and both have strange, almost unbelievable adventures in Venice.

more or less nearly to the ideal. Laws and other social institutions, it is claimed, have improved man's chances by protecting order, property and the rights of the individual, and by rewarding merit and punishing crime. But is this happiness, based on fear, superior to that which man might have attained in the golden age so often described by poets, when love was the only law for mankind, when humanity, still in its infancy, throve unembarrassed by artificially created rules and restrictions?

Having thus propounded the question, he now begins to discuss it from many different angles.

The first poem read in the *Accademia* treated the following argument: "Laws of human society have increased the number of fears and hopes; therefore, because of them, man has been driven further away from happiness." It was a Latin elegy, beginning:

> Ergo ego semotae tactus telluris amore
> Natales potui deseruisse domos? etc.

After this, a long composition in blank verse was recited on the subject: "Man cannot be happy in life, he can only wish to be; and since this desire exists equally in all men whether in a social or a natural state, laws cannot contribute to real happiness." This poem[11] has passages not unworthy of a good poet, as the following, which in style and conception so much resembles the manner followed later by Aleardi:

> Forsennato mortal! fra tai deliri
> Chè l' error tuo non scerni? Indarno stimi
> Fatto il mondo a te sol, vibri sua luce
> Il sol per te, per te s' adorni il campo
> Di bionda messe, e di viole il prato,
> E nell' aria, e nel mar provvida legge

---

[11] It was published for the first time in the *Saggi Poetici*.

> Mille per te animali alberghi e nutra.
> Ma che fanno per te quelle rotanti
> Stelle, che ornano il ciel; nei boschi ircani
> Quella tigre che fa, tanto nemica
> Dell' uman sangue; nei marini gorghi
> L' orca e il delfino, e nella terra il serpe?
> Pur tu ben sai che da una mano stessa
> Uscir tutte quest' opre, e in quel gran tutto
> Che forma l' Universo il proprio loco
> Han queste parti ancor, tanto remote
> Da l' uso de' mortali; a l' uomo il mondo
> Serve, e l' uom serve il mondo, in quella forma
> Che dal mar vien la fonte, e poi nel mare
> Tributaria ritorna; e se fra gli altri
> Membri il grado più eccelso a te concesse
> Libera Provvidenza, a te non lice
> Indagar la cagion, o d' altrui dono
> Darne il merto a te stesso; apri l' orecchio
> A natura che parla; ella ti grida
> Che un sol punto è tua vita, un breve punto
> Che tu stesso non senti.

The third poem was an anacreontic in which this theme was developed: "Man cannot reach happiness by following the impulses of his heart, for he is prevented from so doing by laws; therefore the latter have widened the distance between him and happiness."

Queer theories (one might be tempted to call them Bolshevist nowadays) are advanced in this composition, which however, as Marchesan remarks,[12] does not lack a certain grace. After having denied the usefulness of any law, and, among other things, challenged the right of a father to refuse his daughter's hand to the man whom she loves, that of the state to compel military service, and that of society

---

[12] L. Da Ponte, p. 61. It may be noted in passing that Da Ponte was wise enough not to include this poem in his Saggi Poetici.

to require of a man who likes only gambling and singing, that he should work in order to earn his bread, he concludes with these lines:

> La natura dentro il petto
> Una legge sol mi diè,
> Di non far in atto o in detto
> Quel che poi non piace a me.
>
> Dunque solo in questo seno
> Questa legge in me vivrà,
> E tu poi da un duro freno
> Cerca pur felicità.

In contrast to the eccentricity of the foregoing poem, a gloomy conception of life pervades the *canzone* which comes next, and which is based on this assumption: "The approximate happiness which man can attain is not a concrete thing, but a state of mind apt to be wrong: such state of mind can equally be kept in whatsoever condition of life and hence laws neither afford nor deny means whereby happiness can be reached."[13]

What a Leopardian pessimism, for instance, in this stanza:

> Così per vari modi
> Ciascun muove a quel bene,
> Onde spera quaggiù farsi felice:
> Nè per mirar come se stesso frodi
> Il proprio affetto, viene
> Che sterpi unqua dal cor l' alta radice;
> Chè se trovar non lice
> Che un sommo bene, e più cercarne è vano,
> O fra l' immenso stuolo
> Fora beato un solo,
> O l' integro tesor si chiede invano;
> Ma cieco è l' intelletto, e il ben che agogna
> Nel suo medesmo error si finge, e sogna.

[13] This poem was included in the *Saggi Poetici*.

Fifth in order comes a Latin ode of extraordinary elegance, which is here reproduced in its entirety, for it gives an opportunity of admiring the exquisite taste of our young Poet and his astonishing facility in handling with perfect mastery the Horatian strophe. It treats the following argument: "Happiness is in proportion to wealth: the laws of society distribute wealth unequally thereby rendering happiness more easily attainable for some, and less for others."

> Miraris, Licini, quod nec equo potens
> Threicio, Zephyris ocyor, aut Noto,
> Non crines balano mollior, aut manu
> Stipatus juvenum ferar;
>
> Quem nuper pateras, grataque munera
> Ponentem superis, signaque ahenea,
> Quem nuper Venerem munere videras
> Placantem, ut facilem jocis
>
> Praeberet placida fronte Licorida,
> Cui longum Attalico marmore lucida
> Sedas enituit. Nunc neque purpuram
> Deducunt famulae manus,
>
> Auratumve trabes urget hymettias
> Tectum. Jam galea Mars adamantina,
> Civilique rigens sanguine, barbaris
> Junxit pectora legibus.
>
> Cedunt Vandalico jugera militi
> Nostris ah toties versa ligonibus,
> Ut tristes vacuo nos lare deserant
> Duri foedera consulis.
>
> Infelix platano non ego sub levi
> Posthac hospitium, non violaria
> Quaeram, nec viridem sub juga lauream
> Labentem prope rivulum.
>
> At vos e gelidis collibus insitae
> Vites pampineis crescite brachiis,
> Flavas vimineis ut calathis ferus
> Uvas advena colligat.

Et tu compositis quercubus addita
 Myrtus, jam dominis suesce novis novam
 Porrexisse comam; me trepidum cito
 Pellunt classica murmure.

Jam dira increpitant jura, nec imperi
 Immutare licet foedus, et abditum
 Legum consilium: sic Capitolii
 Clamant culmina verticis.

Sic magna attenuant, sic nova proferunt,
 Summisque ima valent foedera vertere.
 Recte hoc terrigenis afferat alma lex,
 An contra? hoc Superi vident.

The remaining ten compositions, showing more or less the same qualities and faults as those already mentioned, and all treating the same argument from widely different points of view, are:

(1) a poem in *terza rima* defending a theory contradicting that of the Latin ode, viz., "the rich are not happier than the poor;"

(2) a *sermone* in the style of those of Gozzi, not lacking great spontaneity of inspiration and elegance of verse, but extreme in its daring: it violently attacks the privileged classes for claiming rights that they do not have by nature, and supports the contention that humanity enslaved itself the moment it submitted to laws;

(3) a Latin *carmen* of no less than 193 lines, developing the idea that "a king is not happier than his subjects;"

(4) a sonnet in which it is deplored that poverty prevents the education of many gifted minds;

(5) a *capitolo* in *terza rima,* in the style of Berni, in which, not without humor, the reverse argument of the foregoing is presented, viz., "the learned man is not happier than the ignorant;"

(6) Latin hendecasyllables supporting the paradoxical statement that since laws punish vice, they encourage it;

(7) a poem in *ottava rima,* perhaps one of the best for conception, style and facility of verse, which, in opposition to the main contention, affirms that laws are a necessity since human frailty requires them;

(8) an eclogue, in which two shepherds, Silvio and Linco, conversing about the necessity of having laws, agree that, while they do not increase human happiness, they were an unavoidable evil at the beginning of society;

(9) a poem of thanks, also in the form of a pastoral dialogue;

(10) an anacreontic, also of thanks, which seems especially addressed to the prelate who presided at the *Accademia.*[14]

Even nowadays, in an age of democracy and freedom, a subject like that handled by Da Ponte would hardly seem appropriate for discussion among young men destined to become priests. To attempt it then, in the year of grace 1776, in a seminary, in the presence of the Bishop and high church dignitaries, and, as there is reason to believe, also before authorities of that most conservative of all governments, the Republic of St. Mark,—was more than temerity, it was a challenge; and the results were immediate and most disastrous for the unwise young abbé.

The matter was denounced by Father Giuseppe Frassen, the inquisitor, to the magistrate of the *Riformatori,* a kind of ministry of public instruction which the Republic of Venice had instituted as far

---

[14] The poems which in this enumeration bear the numbers (1), (2), (3) and (5) were included in the *Saggi Poetici.*

back as the year 1516, in advance of any other European country.[15] From the *Riformatori,* who, Da Ponte remarks, "had more need to be reformed than morality and judgment for reforming,"[16] the accusation was referred to the Senate, and that body, after investigating further and twice calling the rector of the Seminary of Treviso *ad audiendum verbum,* set December 14th as the date of the trial.

Da Ponte, who up to the end of September had remained in Treviso awaiting developments, was then advised by the family Giustiniani, to which, as has been seen, the Bishop belonged, to go in person to Venice to assume his own defense. Probably it was the same family which furnished him with an introduction to the patrician Bernardo Memmo,[17] whom he says he had the good luck of meeting soon after his arrival in that city.[18] But neither his protection, nor that of the other nobleman, Pietro Zaguri,[19] and not even that of Gaspare Gozzi, who all took a lively interest in his case, could appease the implacable

[15] Centelli, *L. Da Ponte.*
[16] *Memorie,* vol. i, p. 42.
[17] Bernardo Memmo (1730-'97?) belonged to one of the noblest families of Venice, which claimed descent from that Tribuno Memmo who was Doge from 979 to 991. He was a man of talent and broad erudition, and a close friend of Goldoni, who dedicated his *L' uomo di mondo* to him and his more famous brother Andrea (1729-93).
[18] *Memorie,* vol. i, p. 42.
[19] Pietro Antonio Zaguri (1733-1805) was the head of a family, originally of Cattaro (Dalmatia), which had been inscribed in the Golden Book in 1653. Though assuming the rôle of a critic in literature and the arts, nothing remains of him worthy of remembrance. Yet he was a man of uncommon mentality and education, and especially deserves praise for having protected men of letters like Da Ponte and Giacomo Casanova, for whom he felt a deep attachment and to whom he remained a constant friend throughout life. See the introduction of Molmenti to his *Carteggi Casanoviani, Lettere del patrizio Zaguri a G. Casanova* (Palermo, Sandron, 1917) pp. V-XXXIX.

Riformatori. Gozzi, whose reputation in the field of letters was very high at that time and whose advice was of great weight, tried to show that tolerance would be the best policy, and to point out that the man they had to judge had exceptional talents. "So much the worse," they answered him. "We must then render him incapable of doing further harm."[20]

The trial was held on the appointed date, and the most objectionable passages of the *Accademia* were recited with great emphasis before the scandalized magistrates. The following lines from the *sermone* (the seventh poem) caused more indignation than all the rest, for the allusion to the *corna aurate* was interpreted as an outrage to the Doge and to the majesty of the Republic:

> Io di censore
> O di console irato i fasci e il ciglio
> Minaccioso non temo, io d' un sol guardo
> Miro i regi sul trono e per le piazze
> Il cencioso mendico, a cui talvolta
> Porgo vile moneta, onde l' imbarco
> Paghi al nocchier della letea palude.
> Il garrir de' signor, che pien d' orgoglio
> Ergon le corna aurate, un lieve fischio
> Parmi d' aura nascente, e mentre loro
> Prestano omaggio le divote torme,
> Io con equabil ciglio in me raccolto,
> Or la gru passeggiera, or per le nubi
> Qualche mostro volante, ed ora i marmi
> Di Pasquin, di Marforio intento miro.

As a result, Da Ponte was expelled from his position in the Seminary of Treviso and forbidden to teach in any of the schools under the jurisdiction of the *Serenissima*.[21]

[20] *Memorie*, vol. i, p. 43.
[21] For documents relating to the trial, see Marchesan, *L. Da Ponte*, pp. 76-94.

POET AND LIBERTINE

This, however, did not prevent him from remaining in Venice, where he accepted the hospitality generously offered him by Bernardo Memmo, in whose home, we are told in the *Memorie*,[22] he spent a few delightful months. Introduced by his protector and by Pietro Zaguri into the best circles, he was cordially received; the scandal evidently had made him more popular than ever. And it was in that society that he met the famous Giacomo Casanova,[23] as well as the noted *improvvisatori*, Mgr. Stratico (1732-99), Abbé B. Lorenzi (1732-1822), and G. Altanesi (?-1783), whose success tempted him and his brother Girolamo —who also had left Treviso—to try their luck in that line, in which both attained a certain reputation.

In the spring of 1777 the cordial relations between Memmo and Lorenzo came to an abrupt end, through an intrigue which our Poet relates with minute details in his autobiography, claiming that he was an inno-

---

[22] Vol. i, p. 46.
[23] Giacomo Casanova (1725-98) was one of the most interesting types of the class of adventurers so numerous in his time. Born of a family of actors, yet destined to the priesthood, he early in life started on a notorious career which led him to all the capitals of Europe, where, using his exceptional talents with a most unscrupulous code of morals, he lived by gambling, swindling and intrigues. He was alternately an honored guest of the reigning courts and a prisoner or an exile. He acted as an agent for Louis XV and as a spy for the Venetian Republic, while knowing intimately most of the important people of Europe, including the Empress Catherine, Madame de Pompadour, Voltaire, Haller, etc. His almost miraculous escape from the *Piombi* of Venice he described in a book which reads like a romance. Imprisoned in France, England and Spain, expelled from most of the countries of Europe, he retired in his old age to Dux, Bohemia, where he was the librarian of the Count of Waldstein. There he wrote in French his autobiography, the authenticity and sincerity of which have been established by recent investigations. Benedetto Croce has lately declared it to be one of the most precious archives of the XVIII century.

cent victim.[24] Briefly, his story runs thus: a young woman, Teresa by name, with whom Memmo was madly in love and who occupied in his household more or less the position of a mistress, having become jealous of the influence that Da Ponte had acquired over her protector, conspired with a young man, to whom with Memmo's consent she was engaged, to oust the intruder from the Memmo home. It happened that the plot was overheard by Lorenzo late one night, as he was about to retire, and the next morning, greatly excited, he revealed it to his host. Memmo thought he must have dreamed it, but when during the day Teresa treated Da Ponte with marked insolence before guests, the break came and the Poet left the house at once and departed for Padua.

Only subsequently, on his return to Venice, six or seven weeks later, did he learn from a common friend that the woman had accused him to Memmo of having tried to make love to her, and that the latter had believed her. He tried then to convince Memmo of his innocence, but this was no easy matter, and he succeeded only later, when he had the wicked Teresa retract her accusation.

Now, after what we know of our abbé and his avowed weakness for the fair sex, is it unreasonable to suspect that things may not have occurred quite as he would like us to believe? Living under the same roof with a young and probably attractive woman—and almost next door to her—did he really limit himself, as he tells us, to "pleasant, philosophical conversations" with his host? What soon will be related about other adventures, in which his character will appear in a most discreditable light, fully justifies the

---

[24]. *Memorie*, vol. i, pp. 47-49 and 52-55.

suspicion that the causes which led to his sudden departure from Memmo's house were of a more serious nature than he states.

He arrived in Padua with fifty Venetian *lire*[25] as his entire resources. It is true that there he had a brother, Luigi, but the young man, who was then a student at the University of Padua, could hardly have been of any help to him; and a friend who was indebted to him for past favors ungratefully refused him assistance. So he took lodgings in one of the cheapest inns, and for forty-two days his food consisted practically of bread and olives. His poverty, however, did not prevent him from frequenting the cafés, and there he had occasion to meet some of the learned men of the city, among whom was Cesarotti.[26] It was in one of those places that one day he started gambling with students and won a considerable amount of money; with skill and luck on his side, in a few days he had accumulated enough to enable him to return to Venice.

This time it was Pietro Zaguri who opened his house to the Poet, who in his old age gratefully remembered his benefactor as "a nobleman of great learning, a good poet and orator, endowed with fine taste and love for the arts: more generous than rich, more a friend of others than of himself."[27] That he failed to appreciate his good fortune at that time seems however unquestionable, in view of the facts

---

[25] About five dollars.
[26] Melchiorre Cesarotti (1730-1808) was a very prolific writer and a poet of considerable renown. His works, in no less than forty volumes, include, besides original poetry and works on aesthetics, many translations from old and modern languages, among which are justly famous that of Thomas Gray's *Elegy in a Country Churchyard*, and particularly that of *Ossian*.
[27] *Memorie*, vol. i, p. 53.

disclosed by the letters of Zaguri to Casanova, recently published by Molmenti, which throw a very unfavorable light on his character.

It appears from them that the restless abbé, soon after his arrival in Venice, started on a life of intrigues and dissipation, which aroused such a public scandal that eventually Zaguri had to put him out of his house. The passage from the letter of the Venetian nobleman referring to the cause which provoked his action deserves to be quoted, especially since none of Da Ponte's biographers has dwelt on this period of his life.

On October 24th, 1792, Zaguri wrote as follows, evidently in answer to a letter from Casanova informing him of Lorenzo's intention to establish himself in London:

"He is too much of a scoundrel, but, since we also greet scoundrels, greet him in my name. I am perfectly sure that the English will not like him, and that any day some accident will happen to him, such as, after a few months, occurred to him while living in my house, on account of which one fine day I said to him: 'Too many incidents, abbé, too many incidents! This latest one, that of being obliged to assist on a public street a woman pregnant by you, who gave birth on the pavement, I want to be the last I hear from your mouth as long as you live in my house.' And he went to reside with that woman in St. Bartolamio, to the great scandal of the neighborhood."[28]

---

[28] "Egli è troppo briccone, ma come anche i briconi si salutano, salutatelo in mio nome. Credo bene che non piacerà agli inglesi, e ogni dì gli arriverà un accidente, come, dopo alcuni mesi, gli arrivava stando in mia casa, per cui gli dissi un bel giorno: Troppi casi, Ab. troppi casi! Quest' ultimo di dover assistere in strada pubblica una ingravidata da voi, che partorì sulla pietra istriana, desidero che sia l' ultimo caso che intenderò dalla vostra bocca abitante in mia casa.— E se n' andò a far cuzzo con la partoriente a S. Bartolamio, con sururro della contrada." Molmenti, *Cart. Casan.*, vol. ii, pp. 209-10.

POET AND LIBERTINE

That Zaguri did not change the opinion which, after such an unpleasant experience, he had for Lorenzo, is proved by the frequent contemptuous expressions which are found in his letters to Casanova, whenever the name of the abbé occurs. "There can hardly be a worse individual than Da Ponte," he wrote one day, "and I should be tempted to disbelieve whatever he has told you."[29] Then again, in another letter: "Da Ponte is insane in every sense."[30] Finally he gave of the Poet the following description: "A strange man, known to be a rascal of moderate talent, with great aptitude for becoming a man of letters and with physical attractions suited to winning love."[31]

But, on the surface at least, the relations between the two men continued to be pleasant, since in his more prosperous days in Vienna Lorenzo addressed the already quoted stanzas to Pietro Zaguri, *patrizio veneto e senatore amplissimo,* while the latter in 1785 tried to have Da Ponte appointed an academician, and furthermore, in 1790, made an effort to obtain for him permission to return, after long years of exile, to the Venetian state.

There will be occasion to speak later in regard to this latter point.

Meanwhile, during the time in which he was in Zaguri's house, and perhaps on his host's recommendation, Da Ponte obtained the charge of tutoring the

---

[29] "Poco di più cattivo soggetto può darsi del Da Ponte ..... Io sarei tentato di credere tutto falso ciò che egli dissevi." Molmenti, *Cart. Casan.*, vol. ii, p. 199.

[30] "Da Ponte è un pazzo in ogni senso." *Ibid.*, p. 203.

[31] "Uno strano uomo; noto per esser canaglia di mediocre spirito con grandi talenti per esser letterato, e fisiche attrattive per esser amato." *Ibid.*, p. 197.

children of Giorgio Pisani (?-1811), mentioned in the *Memorie*[32] as the "Gracchus of Venice."

As a matter of fact, Pisani was one of the leaders of that turbulent faction, composed in great part of destitute patricians called *Barnabotti,* which formed the most venal and corrupt part of the Major Council, and which during that period had the pretence of promoting reforms in the administration of the state, while in reality seeking only personal advantages.

Now the circumstance that a man having the ambition of holding the reins of government should have entrusted his children to the care of a person under sentence, notorious as the author of subversive writings and leading an immoral life, could not escape bitter criticism on the part of the conservatives who were in power; and both the ambitious patrician and Da Ponte—who claims that at that time he was "loved by women, esteemed by men, flattered by his protectors and full of good hopes"[33]—were bound to meet with trouble.

A *sonetto codato*[34] in Venetian dialect, which he wrote about the beginning of the year 1779, after the defeat of Pisani, who had tried to be elected *avogador*,[35] aroused the indignation of the *grandi* not only by the violent satire directed at them, but also by its scurrility; and there is no wonder that they

[32] Vol. i, p. 53.
[33] *Memorie*, vol. i, p. 55.
[34] It is a sonnet to which tercets in indefinite number are appended (*coda*). This form of poetry, used almost exclusively for satires, was introduced into English literature by Milton (see his "On the New Forces of Conscience under the Long Parliament"), but he did not attract many imitators.
[35] The office of an *avogador* enjoyed very great consideration; it was his business to see that all the tribunals did their work smoothly and regularly.

POET AND LIBERTINE

looked for an opportune occasion to get rid of so troublesome a poet.

In his autobiography Lorenzo attributes the main cause of his banishment to these verses and, posing as a poor victim of political persecution, claims that a pretext was found to indict him, on an accusation of having eaten meat on Fridays and of having neglected to hear mass on Sundays.[36] But this momentous event of his life has recently been cleared up by the discovery of important documents in the State Archives of Venice,[37] due to the efforts of Fausto Nicolini, who, in one of his admirable notes to the Laterza edition of the *Memorie,* brings out the real causes of Da Ponte's exile.[38]

On May 29th, 1779, in the mouth of the lion at San Moisè, was found an anonymous denunciation which bluntly and ungrammatically, after dealing generically with "the horrid and enormous crimes and scandals" daily committed by our abbé, who had embraced the faith "only to trample on it and ridicule it," came to the specific charge against him of adultery. He was accused of having seduced a married woman and of living and procreating with her "in scorn of the sacraments," thus plunging into disgrace "two honorable families whose only shield is their reputation."

As for the persons involved in this scandal, the Poet's autobiography itself gives the clue. Towards the middle of the book, in relating the incidents of a journey he made to Italy years after, he mentions a "very pretty and charming" Florentine woman by the name of Angioletta, wife of a certain Bellaudi,

[36] *Memorie*, vol. i, pp. 56-59.
[37] *Esecutori contro la bestemmia, Processi, anno* 1779. *busta* xxxvi.
[38] *Memorie*, vol. ii, p. 273.

asserting that previous to his exile he had been living for some time in their home. The man—the information goes on—had a brother-in-law named Gabriello Doria, who was "a spy of the inquisition," and against whom the Poet shows bitter resentment, depicting his character and physical appearance in scornful terms.[39] After this, no great stretch of imagination is required to identify Angioletta as the seduced wife, her brother-in-law as the anonymous denunciator, and the Bellaudis and Dorias as the two families dishonored by Lorenzo. Furthermore, that Angioletta was the same woman assisted on the public street, appears also more than probable in view of Zaguri's statement that the abbé, after that scandalous fact, went to live with his mistress.

A regular prosecution for adultery and public concubinage was instituted against Da Ponte by the *Esecutori contro la bestemmia,* a tribunal which had jurisdiction over such crimes. From June to August, 1779, witnesses were heard and, all search for the accused having proved fruitless, the court pronounced by default, on December 17th of the same year, a sentence (published January 5th, 1780, in Venice and a few days later in Ceneda), according to which "Padre Lorenzo Da Ponte" was banished for fifteen years from Venice and dependent territories, and threatened with seven years imprisonment in a dungeon if he were apprehended.

The Poet, forewarned of the impending danger, had left the *ingrata patria* long before the search for him was started, and had taken refuge in Austrian territory.

[39] *Memorie,* vol. i, pp. 217-19 and 226-29.

CHAPTER III

How Da Ponte Became a Librettist

After what has just been narrated, it is not altogether surprising to note that our Poet, when he wrote his autobiography, tried to create an alibi for himself so as to protect his character against any possible rumor of his youthful errors. Accordingly, he states that he arrived in Gorizia on September 1st, 1777, "that is," he adds, "before having reached my twenty-ninth year."[1]

Surely the assertion seems quite definite; but even without taking into account all that has been said towards the end of the preceding chapter, the fact that Lorenzo is not telling the truth is revealed in the next few pages of the *Memorie,* wherein, forgetting himself, he alludes to an historical event the date of which disproves his previous statement and determines beyond doubt the real time in which his flight to Gorizia took place.[2]

A few days after he had arrived in that city, he informs us, the news reached there that the Peace of Teschen had been concluded between Austria and Prussia:[3] this event occurred on May 13th, 1779.[4]

---

[1] *Memorie,* vol. i, p. 64.
[2] Credit must be given to Fausto Nicolini for having first noticed, in his notes to the *Memorie,* this important discrepancy.
[3] *Memorie,* vol. i, p. 68.
[4] If, after this, a further proof be needed to support the above contention, the reader is referred to the already quoted stanzas to Pietro Zaguri, composed by Da Ponte in Vienna

Nor is this the only instance in which the chronology of Da Ponte's adventurous life, as given by him, conflicts with facts mentioned in his book. Other cases, to which the reader's attention will soon be called, confirm the opinion that not too much reliance can be placed on our Poet's assertions.

With a bundle containing part of a suit of clothes, some linen and a few books as his only luggage, he entered on the evening of his arrival in Gorizia the first inn he chanced upon, and met there a very pretty young hostess, whose charms of course he could not resist, and with whom he at once started an idyl under circumstances which Tuckerman calls "as good as a play."[5] The woman, a German or more probably a Slovene,[6] was unable to speak a word of Italian, and her conversation with our gallant abbé was carried on through gestures and by means of a diminutive German and Italian dictionary. After ten or twelve days, during which his only occupation seems to have been that of playing the leading rôle in this agreeable comedy, he decided to leave the inn, since his purse was almost empty and his pride did not permit him to accept the hospitality and financial aid eagerly of-

---

immediately after the fiasco of the first opera for which he wrote a libretto, *Il ricco d' un giorno*, and dealing with the circumstances which caused its failure. The poem contains the following lines:

> Con la fame, col freddo e con l' inedia
> Valoroso pugnai quattr' anni e più.

Il ricco d' un giorno having been given for the first time in the early months of 1784, the "four years and more" of struggle with poverty to which the lines allude bring us back exactly to the year 1779.

[5] *Lorenzo Da Ponte*, in *Putnam's Magazine*, vol. xii (July-December, 1868), pp. 527-36.

[6] "Per mia disgrazia non parlava che tedesco o cragnolino." *Memorie*, vol. i, p. 64.

HOW DA PONTE BECAME A LIBRETTIST 43

fered him by his engaging hostess. So at least he says. Almost penniless, but having acquired quite a vocabulary of German love expressions, which, according to his rather frank admission, was destined to prove a valuable asset in his further adventures "in that city and elsewhere,"[7] he went to live in a miserable little room in the house of a poor family.

Solely from his lyre the Poet hoped now to derive the help he so badly needed. The Peace of Teschen, just spoken of, had been negotiated and signed in the name of Maria Theresa by Count Johann Philipp von Cobenzl (1741-1810), whose father, the old Count Guido, was one of the leading noblemen of Gorizia. That the latter, evidently proud of his son's success, might welcome a poetical glorification of it, was at once perceived by Da Ponte, who accordingly wrote an ode eulogizing the aged Empress and her brilliant diplomat,—ode which he entitled *La gara degli uccelli*, (The Birds' Rivalry), an allusion to the Austrian and Prussian eagles.

Though on more than one occasion Lorenzo showed a paternal predilection for this offspring of his Muse, it is certainly not one of the best of his poems. Yet it sufficed to gain for him the protection of the wealthy patrician, who had it printed at his own expense, and generously rewarded its author. The reputation he thus acquired in the town procured him new favors. Count Rodolfo Coronini (1731-91) entrusted him with a translation into Italian verse of his *Liber primus fastorum Goritiensium,* a work of pretended historical erudition,—the *Fasti Goriziani* alluded to in the *Memorie.* Other families, all equally prominent, such as those of Strassoldo, Lantieri, Attems, Tuns and Tor-

[7] *Memorie*, vol. i, p. 67.

riani, opened their doors to him, and the young poet soon became a favorite in that society.

It happened, however, that his uncommon good luck aroused envy in another poet, Giuseppe de Colletti (1744-1815), whom Lorenzo describes in his autobiography with the bitterest animosity and against whom he wrote at that time a violent satire.[8]

Meanwhile, at the request of a noble lady, he translated, probably through the French, a German tragedy for the use of a good Italian theatrical company which was giving performances in Gorizia. The play, he freely admits, proved a failure, but his reputation was somewhat restored when, shortly after, another production of his was presented,—this time the translation of a French tragedy.[9] Admitted to an "Arcadic colony" which had just then been founded in Gorizia under the name of *Colonia Sonziaca* (a designation derived from that of the river Isonzo on which that city is situated), he had himself called *Lesbonico Pegasio*. Among the poems composed by him for that society, *Il capriccio* and *La gratitudine o sia la difesa delle donne* deserve to be remembered.[10]

Yet, despite his remarkable success, it appears that he was far from happy, and in his heart he longed for a return to the City of the Lagoons. If he entertained any hope that his old protector, Giorgio Pisani,

---

[8] It does not seem true that Colletti was such an ignoramus as our Poet would like us to believe. Disregarding his poetical work, which in fact was hardly better than amateurish, it may be mentioned that he founded in Trieste, some years later, the *Osservatore Triestino*, and from 1791 to his death he held the position of public librarian in that city. See Nicolini in his notes to the *Memorie* (vol. ii, p. 275).

[9] Nothing more definite is known about the German tragedy, not even its title. The tragedy translated from French is *Warwick*, by J. F. de La Harpe (1739-1803).

[10] They were published for the first time in Gorizia (1780), and then again in the *Saggi Poetici*.

might grasp the reins of the Venetian government and recall him, that hope was rudely shattered by the news brought to him by Caterino Mazzolà,[11] whom he had known in the house of Memmo, and who passed through Gorizia on his way to Dresden, where at the invitation of that Elector he was about to assume the position of Poet for the Opera House.

Pisani, he was told, after having been elected by popular vote *Procuratore di San Marco,* had one night been arrested by order of the Inquisition and, without trial, imprisoned in Verona.[12] Realizing then that there was no prospect of an end to his banishment, Lorenzo entreated his more fortunate friend to recommend him for a position at the Court of Saxony. This Mazzolà promised to do, and hardly had two months elapsed when a letter purporting to be from him reached Da Ponte with the request that he start at once for Dresden.

Everybody, even Colletti, with whom meanwhile he had come to friendly terms, seemed grieved at his departure, and during an entertainment held in the

[11] Caterino Mazzolà (?-1806), "colto e leggiadro poeta," says Da Ponte (*Memorie*, vol. i, p. 52), "ed il primo forse che seppe scrivere un dramma buffo," was born of a distinguished Venetian family in Longarone nel Cadore, and educated in Treviso. He acquired quite a reputation not only as a poet but also as a man of uncommon erudition; was a Poet at the Court of Saxony and later at that of Vienna, and wrote a considerable number of melodramas, among which especially noteworthy are: *Il marito indolente* (1782), *Il capriccio corretto* (1783), *Il pazzo per forza* (1783), and *Amore giustificato* (1794).

[12] Da Ponte states that Mazzolà came to Gorizia eight months after his own arrival in that city (*Memorie*, vol. i, p. 73). His chronology would then fix the time of this visit around May, 1778. But the election of Giorgio Pisani occurred on March 8th, 1780, and his arrest only three months after that date; therefore the passage of Mazzolà through Gorizia must have taken place during the summer or early autumn of 1780.

house of one of his protectors the evening before he left—New Year's Eve, by the way—a fairly large sum was collected among the guests and gracefully offered to him as a farewell gift.

In Vienna, as he states, he arrived soon after the death of Maria Theresa.[13] The gay City of the Danube, which had been deeply attached to the aged empress, was transformed into a city of sorrow and gloom: Da Ponte spent only three days there, during which he was received by Cobenzl, from whose father he had obtained a letter of introduction and by whom he was presented with another gift of one hundred florins.

On his arrival in Dresden, however, instead of the warm welcome he had anticipated, he was received by Mazzolà with nothing but expressions of great surprise, and it did not take him long to discover that the letter which had induced him to leave Gorizia had never been written by his friend and was only a cruel hoax perpetrated by some enemy. As to who this could be, no doubt remained in his mind after recalling that he had spoken to his self-styled friend Colletti of the promise that Mazzolà had given him on leaving Gorizia: the wily man had taken revenge for the satire which Lorenzo had written against him and, at the same time, had eliminated his rival.[14] Mazzolà promised to do all he could for him and in the mean-

---

[13] *Memorie*, vol. i, p. 76. The death of Maria Theresa occurred on November 29th, 1780, and thus Da Ponte's stay in Gorizia lasted altogether one year and eight months. His mentioning this other historical event brings still further proof of the incorrectness of the date he gives of his arrival in Gorizia.

[14] This is the version given in the *Memorie* (vol. i, pp. 76-77). Whether or not the facts were as Da Ponte relates them there is no way to ascertain, since we have only his word for it.

time treated him with cordial hospitality. Through him Lorenzo met some distinguished men, among them Count Marcolini,[15] a personal friend and minister of the Elector, and the learned ex-Jesuit, Father Huber.[16]

In order partially to repay the favors he was receiving, Da Ponte offered to collaborate with Mazzolà in the composition of the plays which the latter was preparing for that Opera House, a help which it seems was gladly accepted. It was for our Poet, as he soon had occasion to discover, a sort of training for his future career.

But, apart from this work, his residence in Dresden and the close association with a pious man like Father Huber inspired him to compose a number of "psalms" which rank among his best poems. They are not, as some of his biographers[17] have erroneously surmised, translations of the Psalms of David, but

---

[15] Count Camillo Marcolini (1736-1824) was born in Fano and belonged to a prominent Italian family. After spending his early youth in his native town, he was sent to Vienna to complete his studies, and afterwards as a page to the Court of Saxony. Having gained, through years of close association with the Elector, his affection and confidence, he was appointed minister and played an important rôle in the relations of his prince with Napoleon. He fostered the porcelain industry in Dresden, and introduced into that part of Germany the cultivation of silkworms. Molmenti, *Cart. Casan.*, vol. i, p. 268.

[16] Michael Huber (1748-1811), a native of German Tyrol, was in fact a man of unusual erudition. He had a perfect knowledge of Italian and translated into German Metastasio's *La morte di Abele* and *La Passione*, under the title *Gedichte von P. M. aus dem italienischen ins deutsche übersetzt* (Sommervogel, *Bibliothèque de la Compagnie de Jésus*, vol. iv, p. 508).

[17] Samuel Ward, *Sketch of the Life of Lorenzo Da Ponte*, published for the first time in the *New York Mirror* (August, 1838), and republished in pamphlet form, dedicated to Dr. John W. Francis, in New York, October, 1842. Attilio Centelli, *L. Da Ponte*.

original compositions in varying meters, each having as a theme a passage from the Bible, such as *Miserere mei, Deus, quoniam infirmus sum,* or *Iustus es, Domine, et rectum iudicium tuum,* from which he developed the first two poems. For their austere simplicity coupled with unusual elegance of style, they were praised by many men of letters and, as Da Ponte with pardonable pride informs us,[18] by no less an authority than Ugo Foscolo. Both Father Huber, to whom the verses were dedicated, and the Elector, who was presented with them by the learned clergyman, generously rewarded our Poet.

If the reader, however, imagines that Lorenzo, repenting his past sins, had undergone a sincere conversion, he will be speedily disillusioned by reading in what an entanglement he became involved and how, in order to extricate himself, he was obliged to depart abruptly from Dresden.

The publication of these "psalms" had brought him into contact with many cultured persons, among whom was an Italian artist in whose home Lorenzo became a welcome visitor. The man had two lovely daughters, and a wife still youthful and attractive: our abbé fell in love with both girls at the same time, while not neglecting to pay flattering attention to the mother as well. Seeing that the affair threatened to take a dangerous turn, for, at least as far as the girls were concerned, they both seemed infatuated with him, the artist's wife asked the poet to choose between marrying one of them or ceasing his visits.

Later in that same evening Da Ponte was in his room trying to find a way out and unable to decide what answer to give, when Mazzolà entered bringing

[18] *Memorie,* vol. i, p. 80.

him a letter from home in which his old father informed him of the death of his brother Luigi. Though the news was not entirely unexpected, for he was aware that the young man was suffering from a serious illness, his grief was bitter; in vain Mazzolà tried to console him, and finally, in an attempt to divert his mind from his sorrow, he read to him in a half-serious way a letter he himself had received, in which some friend in Venice warned him to watch Da Ponte lest he usurp his position in the Dresden Opera House. To the supersensitive poet it appeared as if his friend really entertained that suspicion, and this, added to his other troubles, led him to the impulsive decision of leaving that city at once. While Mazzolà was still with him, he wrote a short note to Father Huber informing him of his plan and asking to be allowed to take leave of him early the next morning.

It is more than possible that Mazzolà was somewhat relieved at the idea of his going; but proof that he still wished to help his friend is furnished by the fact that he advised him to go to Vienna, where his talents might win recognition, and moreover provided him with a letter of introduction to Salieri,[19] who at that time was one of the leading operatic composers, and enjoyed the favor of Emperor Joseph II.

[19] Antonio Salieri (1750-1825) was a native of Legnano. Through the family Mocenigo he obtained free admission in the choir school of St. Mark's in Venice. In 1766 he was taken to Vienna by F. L. Gassmann, who introduced him to Joseph II. His first opera, *Le donne letterate*, was produced at the Burg-Theater in 1770. On Gassmann's death (1774) he became *Kapelmeister*, and held his office for fifty years though he made frequent visits to Italy and France. His *chef d'œuvre* was *Axur, re d'Ormus* (libretto by Da Ponte), a work which the public of Vienna preferred to Mozart's *Don Giovanni*. Salieri gave lessons in composition to Cherubini and Beethoven, who dedicated to him "Three Sonatas for Pianoforte and Violin," Op. 12.

With this letter and generous gifts, including a fur coat and one hundred florins in gold, presented to him by Father Huber, after an affectionate farewell interview, Da Ponte set forth for the Austrian capital. This occurred towards the end of 1781 or the beginning of 1782, when he was about thirty-three year old.[20]

It does not seem that at first he met with extraordinary success in Vienna. From Salieri all he probably obtained was some vague promise, for it was only later that the composer appears to have taken important steps in his behalf.

Da Ponte was living on the money he had brought with him and, as he was still unable to speak German fluently, he associated only with Italians. One of his new friends, at whose suggestion he had composed and dedicated to "a very high personage" a delightful poem on an old Ovidian theme, *Filemone e Bauci*, found an occasion to bring the verses to the attention of the more than octogenarian Metastasio, who was so favorably impressed by them that he requested that the young author be presented to him.

One has only to recall the unbounded admiration felt by Da Ponte for the famous poet ever since his childhood, to imagine with what a thrill he approached him and received his praise. Before a numerous audience the poem was read, in part by Metastasio himself, in part by Lorenzo, and was greatly admired.[21]

---

[20] Assumed from the fact that, in Vienna, Da Ponte met Metastasio and that the latter died on April 12th, 1782.

[21] Da Ponte relates in his *Memorie* (vol. i, pp. 93-94) an interesting fact concerning the death of the old Caesarean Poet, which occurred soon after his interview with him. It seems that Joseph II decided one day to abolish the numerous pensions that Maria Theresa during her long reign had bounteously scattered around at the expense of the State.

ANTONIO SALIERI
FROM AN ENGRAVING BY J. NEIDL, AFTER A PORTRAIT BY
STEINHAUSER VON TREUBERG, AT THE HOF-
BIBLIOTHEK IN VIENNA.

HOW DA PONTE BECAME A LIBRETTIST

The problem of his means of existence, however, still remained unsolved, and we may easily suppose that his economic difficulties were as bad as ever when he tells us that he found it necessary to move to one of the poorest suburbs, where for "many months" he lived mainly on borrowed money.[22]

Yet his lucky star was about to rise. Towards the end of that year (1782), having learned that the Emperor intended to establish an Italian theatre in Vienna, he boldly approached Salieri, asking that he be recommended for a position similar to that held by Mazzolà in Dresden. Salieri took the matter to heart, spoke to Count Olindo Orsini di Rosemberg (1725-96), High Chamberlain and intimate friend of Joseph II, and the request was granted.

In his account of his first audience with the Emperor, Da Ponte relates that he was asked whether he had ever written a drama. To his frank denial Joseph answered good-naturedly: "Never mind, we shall have a virgin Muse!"[23]

The title conferred on him was that of "Poet to the Italian Theatre," and he received a yearly salary of 1200 florins, with the obligation of writing dramas, for which, according to usage, he was in addition to receive royalties.

To the poor man, whose life since his flight from Venice had been a daily struggle for existence, this sudden change bringing to him at the same time comforts and honors, must have seemed like a golden dream. He obtained at once access to the best homes

---

Metastasio felt so keenly this act, which he interpreted as a lack of gratitude for his long service and an insult to his merit, that he became ill and died without learning that the Emperor had made an exception in his case.

[22] *Memorie*, vol. i, p. 94.
[23] *Ibid.*, vol. i, p. 95.

of the Austrian capital and became acquainted with men elevated in rank or prominent in the fields of art, by whom he was treated with esteem and benevolence. It was at this early stage of his theatrical career that he met, in the house of Baron Wetzlar, the already famous Mozart.

It is curious to read in the *Memorie* of the difficulties which he encountered in writing his first melodrama, *Il ricco d' un giorno*. To quote his words, it seemed to him as though he had undertaken "to wield the club of Hercules with a child's hand."[24] For many months he struggled with his subject, and only towards the end of 1783 was he able to submit the completed libretto to Salieri, who had to compose the music.

In that period he was greatly saddened by the news of the death, on August 8th,[25] of his brother Girolamo, to whom he was so deeply attached and whose advice had so often been of invaluable aid to him. An incurable malady of the lungs had carried him away, at the age of thirty-one, when he was one of the chief supporters of his father's large family. This responsibility now fell on Lorenzo; and it was not a trifling one, for no less than three boys and nine girls[26] had been the outcome of his father's second marriage.

[24] *Memorie*, vol. i, p. 97.
[25] This date appears in the death registers of Ceneda, as discovered by Marchesan (*L. Da Ponte*, p. 486).
[26] Only seven sisters are mentioned in the *Memorie* when the Poet describes his return to Ceneda in 1798, after many years of exile (vol. i, p. 212). But in his *epistola* to Casti, written in 1786 (*Saggi Poetici*, vol. i, p. 140) he says he had nine:

> Oltre il resto ho un padre vecchio,
> Che non può viver di versi,
> E di più nove sorelle,
> Che non son dee di Parnaso.

Two of them probably died between the time in which he wrote these lines and that of his trip to to his home town.

The music of *Il ricco d' un giorno* was composed by Salieri during the early spring of 1784. Unfortunately the opera could not be given at that time, for the composer had to go to Paris for the first performance of his *Le Danaidi,* the score of which he had written in substitution for Gluck. To make matters worse, Casti, whose reputation as a poet was widespread all over Europe, came to Vienna from St. Petersburg in the beginning of May, followed soon after by Paisiello, whose fame in the field of music was at least as great as Salieri's, and the Emperor commanded an opera from them.

When, on August 23d, their *Re Teodoro a Venezia* was given, the great expectations of the sovereign and the public were realized; the opera obtained an extraordinary success, and, while Da Ponte would like us to believe that the applause was only for the music and the singers, it is certain that Casti's share in the triumph was recognized as well.

In the autumn, Salieri having returned, *Il ricco d' un giorno* was finally presented. It proved a complete fiasco. From Da Ponte's stanzas to Pietro Zaguri it appears that the hisses in the theatre were so insistent as to cause the performance to be suspended. Lorenzo, though frankly admitting the faults of his libretto, accuses Salieri of having mutilated it, claims that the music was worse than the words, and finally complains that the great artiste, Storace,[27] being indisposed, her rôle had been entrusted to an incapable singer. There was probably some truth in these as-

[27] Anna Selina Storace (1766-1817), sister of the composer Stefano Storace, was born in London, of Italian parents. She studied in Venice under Sacchini and with her exceptional voice soon became one of the foremost singers of her time. She sang the part of Susanna in the first performance of Mozart's *Le nozze di Figaro.*

sertions, but when Lorenzo goes so far as to accuse Casti of trying to ruin him in order to foster his own ambitions, and of combining with all the adventurous poetasters who at that time crowded Vienna, in a conspiracy headed by no less a personage than Count Rosemberg, it seems that his imagination and his peculiar weakness for seeing rivals and enemies everywhere overpowered his better judgment.

Granting that Casti craved the place left vacant by the death of Metastasio, nothing forbade the simultaneous existence of a "Caesarean Poet" and a "Poet to the Italian Theatre," and therefore it is hard to see why the author of *Gli animali parlanti,* whose happy-go-lucky nature is well known, should have organized so devilish a plot. Even more absurd appears the accusation against Rosemberg (to whom, by the way, he owed his position) for the Count was too much of an Austrian courtier, as Nicolini opportunely remarks,[28] to attempt to persecute a favorite of the Emperor, as Da Ponte undoubtedly was.

Nor is serious consideration due to the matter of a short dialogue in his praise and against Casti which Lorenzo inserted in his *Memorie,*[29] and which is supposed to have taken place between Joseph II and Count Rosemberg the day after the performance of the unlucky opera; for the Venetian ambassador, Daniele Andrea Dolfin (1748-98), to whom the Emperor is said to have related it, and from whom it reached the ear of Da Ponte, was at that time representing the Republic of St. Mark at the Court of France and only on May 20th, 1786, came to Vienna to succeed Sebastiano Foscarini.[30]

[28] Notes to the *Memorie,* vol. ii, p. 278.
[29] Vol. i, p. 103.
[30] Molmenti, *Cart. Casan.,* vol. i, pp. 34 and 245-46.

Be that as it may, Salieri took a solemn oath rather to allow his fingers to be cut off than again to write music for Lorenzo's verses. Nor were the singers more kindly disposed, for they wondered how they could have attempted to sing "those miserable lyrics." Satirical pamphlets were written against our Poet, to which he did not fail to answer with equal violence.[31] The storm, however, was overcome, inasmuch as the Emperor retained him in his favor, and when, towards the beginning of the following year (1785), the two musicians, Stefano Storace[32] and Vincenzo Martini,[33] came to Vienna, he asked Da Ponte to write a libretto for the latter.

But a peculiar accident occurred at this juncture to distract the Poet from his work and seriously to endanger his health. A certain Dorigutti, who practiced surgery in Vienna, being requested by Da Ponte for a remedy against a disturbance of the gums with which he was troubled, took a dastardly revenge on the unsuspecting man, for a supposed love rivalry, by administering to him *aquafortis,* as a result of which

---

[31] *Memorie*, vol. i, p. 102.

[32] Stefano Storace (1763-96), born of Italian parents in London, was sent in his early youth to Naples and educated at the *Conservatorio di Sant' Onofrio*. His first opera, *Gli sposi malcontenti*, was given in Vienna in 1785; afterwards he produced *Gli equivoci*, but his greatest success he achieved in England, on his return in 1787, with his *The Doctor and the Apothecary*, *The Haunted Tower*, *No Song No Supper* and *The Siege of Belgrade*.

[33] Vicente Martin y Solar, self-styled Vincenzo Martini, and known in Italy as *Lo Spagnuolo* (1754-1810) was a native of Valencia. He started his career as a composer in Florence, where his *Ifigenia in Aulide* was given in 1781. Soon after he produced *Astartea*, and, in 1783, *La donna festeggiata* and *L' accorta cameriera*. In 1784, his *Ipermnestra* was produced in Rome. In Vienna, however, he obtained the greatest triumph with *Il burbero di buon cuore*, *La capricciosa corretta*, *L' arbore di Diana* and *Una cosa rara*. In 1788 he was appointed director of the Italian Opera in St. Petersburg.

he lost all his teeth and suffered for over a year from the ill-effects on his digestive organs.

Il burbero di buon cuore, an evident adaptation from the well known comedy of Goldoni, *Le Bourru bienfaisant,* set to music by Martini during the fall of that year, was finally produced on the evening of January 4th, 1786.[34] That the opera was received with exceptional favor, is proved by the fact that for many years it continued to be played in Vienna and was also quite popular in Italy. It seems that Joseph II, on meeting the Poet immediately after the first performance, said to him with a smile: *Abbiamo vinto!*[35]

And undoubtedly Lorenzo's prestige was restored. His popularity had grown overnight to such an extent that several of the foremost composers evidenced a desire to avail themselves of his services as a librettist.

One month later,—to be precise, on February 7th,—in the Court Theatre of Schönbrunn, was produced the musical farce *Le parole dopo la musica,* which, according to a rather curious anecdote related by the

[34] Rob. Eitner, *Biographisch-bibliographisches Quellen-Lexikon der Musiker und Musikgelehrten,* vol. vi, p. 351.

[35] *Memorie,* vol. i, p. 107. In his quaint *Reminiscences,*—a book rich in theatrical information and stage anecdotes, but unfortunately marred by many blunders (from Naples Bay he is able to see "the delightful coast of Tarentum," p. 23—Gaeta he places in Abruzzo, p. 74; not to mention that almost every Italian name he quotes is mis-spelled),—Michael Kelly, famous singer and a composer of some ability, relates that Joseph II "spoke Italian like a Tuscan," and adds: "He came almost every night to the opera, accompanied by his nephew, Francis, then a youth. He usually entered his box at the beginning of the piece, but if not there at the precise moment the curtain was to be drawn up, he had given orders that he was never to be waited for. He was passionately fond of music, and a most excellent and accurate judge of it" (vol. i, pp. 204-5).

HOW DA PONTE BECAME A LIBRETTIST

Prince of Ligne, [36] was written by Casti by order of the Emperor, after the music had already been composed by Salieri.

Michael Kelly (1762-1826), who sang the tenor rôle, gives in his *Reminiscences*[37] an amusing account of the performance and, though by an evident error he attributes the music to Righini[38] (spelled by him *Rigini*) and the words to Da Ponte, the facts related by him must be true since our Poet corroborates them in his *Memorie*.[39]

"There was a character," he says, "of an amorous, eccentric poet, which was allotted to me. At that time, I was esteemed a good mimic, and particularly happy in imitating the walk, countenance and attitudes of those whom I wished to resemble. My friend the poet [*Da Ponte*] had a remarkably awkward gait, a habit of throwing himself (as he thought) into a graceful attitude by putting his stick behind his back and leaning on it; he had also a very peculiar, rather dandyish way of dressing; for, in sooth, the abbé stood mighty well with himself and had the character of a consummate coxcomb; he had also a strong lisp and broad Venetian dialect.

"The first night of the performance, he was seated in the boxes more conspicuously than was absolutely necessary, considering he was the author of the piece to be performed. As usual, on the first night of a new opera, the Emperor was present, and a numerous auditory. When I made my *entrée*, as the amorous poet, dressed like the abbé in the boxes, imitating his walk, leaning on my stick, and aping his gestures and

---

[36] See Marco Landau, *La letteratura italiana alla corte d' Austria*, Aquila, 1880, first Italian translation, p. 88.
[37] Vol. i, p. 233.
[38] Vincenzo Righini (1756-1812), a native of Bologna, enjoyed no mean reputation as a composer. He wrote twenty operas, besides church music, several cantatas and innumerable songs. After a successful career all over Europe, he was from 1793 at the head of the Italian Opera in Berlin.
[39] Vol. i, p. 112.

his lisp, there was a universal roar of laughter and applause; and after a buzz round the house, the eyes of the whole audience were turned to the place where he was seated. The Emperor enjoyed the joke, laughed heartily; the abbé was not at all affronted, but took my imitation of him in good part, and ever after we were on the best terms."

That speaks well for the good nature of our Poet; but his grudge against Casti was certainly aggravated by what he deemed a deliberate caricature of himself.

For Giuseppe Gazzaniga (1743-1819), judged by him "a composer of some merit, but of antiquated style,"[40] he had to prepare soon after a libretto, at the request of Count Rosemberg. The work, undertaken with little enthusiasm, was completed in a few days: it was *Il finto cieco*—an adaptation, as he says, of a French comedy—and was indifferently received.

But for this failure Da Ponte had opportunity soon after to console himself with a new work, the clamorous success of which brought him to the foremost position among living librettists, revealing at the same time the excellence as an operatic composer of that prodigious genius, Wolfgang Amadeus Mozart.

[40] *Memorie*, vol. i, p. 110.

EMPEROR JOSEPH II OF AUSTRIA

FROM AN OLD PRINT.

CHAPTER IV

GLORY AND DOWNFALL

As has been stated, Da Ponte met Mozart for the first time in the early part of 1783, at the home of Baron Wetzlar, a wealthy Jew with whom the great composer was then lodging.[1] That they had already discussed on that occasion the possibility of collaborating on a new opera, appears from the following passage of a letter which Mozart wrote to his father, on May 7th of that year:

"A certain Abbé Da Ponte is our poet here; he has at present a great deal to do in theatrical revision, and has been charged *per obligo* to write a new libretto for Salieri. He will not be able to finish this for two months, after which he has promised to write one for me. But who can tell whether he can or will keep his word? You understand these Italian gentlemen; they are very charming on the surface, but—well, you know what I mean! If he fraternizes with Salieri, I may well wait for the rest of my life for a libretto from him. And yet I should be so glad to show what I can do in an Italian opera."[2]

But Da Ponte, despite this rather pessimistic view, was faithful to his promise and as soon as he could he began to work on the libretto of *Le nozze di Figaro*. Free from any engagement with Salieri after the fiasco of his first production, and eager to gain credit

---

[1] *Memorie*, vol. i, p. 109.
[2] *Die Briefe W. A. Mozarts und seiner Familie, Erste kritische Gesamtausgabe*, by Ludwig Schiedermair (Munich, Müller, 1914) vol. ii, p. 223.

and reputation, our Poet was keen enough to perceive the advantage of allying himself with the young German composer, who, though still a novice in the operatic field,[3] enjoyed already a European renown in the other branches of music.

As he himself states,[4] it was Mozart who suggested that he turn Beaumarchais' *Mariage de Figaro* into an opera. The idea probably originated from the fact that Paisiello's *Barbiere* had recently obtained an extraordinary success in Vienna. Furthermore, there is ground to believe that Mozart, knowing what excitement Beaumarchais' second comedy had created in Paris after having been prohibited for three years,[5] foresaw that the curiosity of the Viennese public would be aroused by a presentation of it in operatic form, and that this would contribute to the success of his work.

The first difficulty which Da Ponte encountered in writing his libretto, was that of treating the subject in such a manner as to preclude the imperial censor from raising any objection to it. In this he showed uncommon ability, for, while eliminating whatever seemed too daring, he faithfully reproduced in his verses the vivacity and delightful humor of the original play.

---

[3] Mozart's operatic production, up to the time in which he composed *Le nozze di Figaro*, consists of youthful attempts which, as Edward J. Dent remarks (*Mozart's Operas*, London, Chatto & Windus, 1913, p. 31), "have a certain interest, as contributing their share towards the gradual growth of his musical personality; but if we look at them merely as forerunners of the great dramas which still hold the stage, we can find little in them that is of permanent and first-rate importance." Among the earlier operas he wrote, the most noteworthy are *Idomedeo* and *Die Entführung aus dem Serrail.*

[4] *Memorie*, vol. i, p. 110.

[5] It was given for the first time on April 27th, 1784.

GLORY AND DOWNFALL

In his *Memorie*[6] he tells us that the score was written by Mozart almost as fast he handed him the words, and that the opera was completed in only six weeks. This explains the gap we find in Mozart's letters just at this period, and a note that Leopold Mozart wrote to his daughter on November 11th, 1785, not only enables us approximately to fix the time in which *Le nozze di Figaro* was composed, but also confirms Da Ponte's statement that the work which they had undertaken was pushed with feverish haste.

"At last," the note says, "I have received a letter of twelve lines from your brother. He apologizes owing to the fact that he is up to his eyes in work finishing *Le nozze di Figaro*. In order to keep his mornings free, he has put off all his pupils to the afternoons."[7]

When the opera was completed Da Ponte undertook to secure the Emperor's consent for its performance. As was to be expected, the first objection made was to the subject; but this difficulty the crafty Poet easily overcame by pointing out that he had transformed Beaumarchais' violent satire into a harmless opera which could give offense to no one. The next obstacle was the fact that Joseph II, as was known, had a strong prejudice against Mozart and held him in slight esteem as an operatic composer. Here again Da Ponte showed his skill. With great tact and subtle diplomacy he informed the Emperor that the score was already completed and suggested that His Majesty, being himself so competent a musician, could form his own opinion as to the merits of the opera by ordering the composer to appear in his presence and play some excerpts.

[6] Vol. i, p. 111.
[7] *Die Briefe W. A. Mozarts*, etc., vol. iv, p. 308.

Highly flattered, Joseph did as the Poet had advised, and the result was that the opera was ordered to be produced.

At this point in his *Memorie,* Lorenzo informs the reader that his "rivals," headed by Casti, who was powerfully protected by Count Rosemberg, tried by every means to spoil the success of the new opera; and he relates the following anecdote: Rosemberg, having learned that in the concluding scene of the third act the peasants assisting at Figaro's wedding were supposed to perform a little dance, took upon himself to interpret literally a command issued by the Emperor some time before, and in a rather blunt manner ordered the Poet to cut out that scene. Mozart was in despair. He intended to appeal directly to the Emperor and threatened to withdraw the score. Da Ponte had a hard time in calming him, and pretending to acquiesce in silence recurred to a clever stratagem in order to attain his purpose: in one of the principal rehearsals given in the presence of the Emperor, when the opera came to its finale and the forbidden scene had to be performed, the orchestra suddenly ceased playing, the singers became dumb and started gesticulating as in a pantomine.—"What's all this?" exclaimed Joseph, turning to Casti, who was sitting behind him.—"Perhaps the poet can tell you, Your Majesty," suggested Casti with a grin. And Lorenzo, summoned into the presence of the Emperor, without saying a word showed him the libretto from which Rosemberg had torn the dance scene. Count Rosemberg had an audience in his turn, was reproved for what he had done, and the ballet was restored.[8]

Almost every biographer of Mozart and of Da Ponte

---

[8] *Memorie,* vol. i, pp. 118-20.

W. A. MOZART

FROM AN ENGRAVING BY KOHL AFTER A MEDALLION BY POSCH, AT THE MOZARTMUSEUM IN SALZBURG.

has accepted this story as an actual occurrence; yet had it really taken place, is it not more than probable that Michael Kelly—who in his *Reminiscences* takes a particular delight in relating all kinds of anecdotes —would have recorded the incident in his book? Considering that he was one of the singers at the first performance of the opera, and that as such he would have taken an active part in the interpolated pantomime or at least have witnessed it, the fact that he makes no mention of it is indeed surprising.

The opera was presented for the first time at the Viennese Court Theatre on May 1st, 1786, with the following cast: Signora Laschi sang the part of the Contessa, Anna Storace that of Susanna, and Frau Gottlieb that of Barbarina, while the baritone Mandini took the rôle of Almaviva, Benucci that of Figaro, Michael Kelly those of Basilio and Don Curzio, and Bussani those of Bartolo and Antonio.

"Never," says Kelly again, "had one beheld such a triumph. The theatre was packed and so many numbers had to be repeated that the time of the performance was nearly doubled."[9]

Yet, despite this immense enthusiasm, the popularity of *Le nozze di Figaro* was not of long duration, and, after nine performances during that season, the opera disappeared from the Vienna stage and was not mounted again until three years later, when, that is, the success of *Don Giovanni* had again brought Mozart into prominence.

Shortly after the production of *Le nozze di Figaro*, our Poet was relieved from the continual fears which had harassed him until now on account of the presence of Casti in Vienna. It seems that Casti, still eager

[9] *Reminiscences*, vol. i, p. 261.

to obtain the appointment as Caesarean Poet, presented his *Poema Tartaro* to Joseph II, hoping thus to attain his end. The result, however, was exactly the reverse of his anticipation, for the Emperor bestowed upon him six hundred sequins with the intimation that he might find them useful in leaving Austria.[10]

With a care-free mind, Lorenzo redoubled his activity. He wrote at this time, for the composer Storace, the libretto of *Gli equivoci,* which he derived from Shakespeare's *Comedy of Errors* and in which, as Kelly remarks, "he retained all the main incidents and characters" of the original play.[11]

But he attained a still greater success with the production, during the autumn of that same year, of *Una cosa rara,* set to music by Martini and undoubtedly the Spanish composer's masterpiece. The source from which Da Ponte took the plot of this opera is, as he states in his *Memorie,*[12] the play *La luna de la Sierra,* which he erroneously attributes to Calderon, while it is by Luis Velez de Guevara, as pointed out by Arturo Farinelli in his exhaustive study on *Don Giovanni.*[13]

Despite some intrigues on the part of the singers, related by our Poet with the usual amount of details which he employs whenever he dwells upon the obstacles he encountered, the new opera obtained a success that overshadowed that of *Le nozze.* Both Da Ponte and the composer became the favorites of

[10] *Memorie*, vol. i, pp. 121-23. There is no doubt that Casti was dismissed in this peremptory manner, for almost all of his biographers, even those who wrote before the publication of Da Ponte's autobiography, concede the fact to be as described by our Poet.

[11] *Reminiscences*, vol. i, p. 233.

[12] Vol. i, p. 124.

[13] *Giornale storico della letteratura italiana*, Turin, 1896, vol. xxvii, pp. 79-81.

Viennese society, while the ladies even adopted the vogue of dressing *à la Cosa Rara*.[14]

Besieged now by several composers, Lorenzo hastily wrote for Righini *Il filosofo punito,* which was produced towards the end of 1786.[15] It was received with marked indifference and, as Lorenzo facetiously remarks,[16] it might better have been entitled "Both the maestro and the poet punished."

Another libretto which he prepared, shortly after, for the Sicilian composer Francesco Piticchio, that of *Bertoldo,* was even less fortunate. The opera, performed for the first time on June 22d of the following year,[17] was a complete failure, and our Poet relates that Joseph II, on meeting him a few days later, gave him the advice not to write any more for composers who were not of the first rank.[18]

The suggestion did not pass unheeded, and when Da Ponte soon after set again to work, he started to write simultaneously a libretto for Mozart, another for Martini, and a third one for Salieri, who, after our Poet's recent triumphs, had reconsidered his former vow and had humbly begged that their past differences might be forgotten.

To the Emperor, who expressed his doubts as to the possibility of carrying out successfully such an arduous task, Lorenzo replied: "I shall try. I will work for Mozart at night and I will picture to myself that I am studying Dante's *Inferno;* I will devote my mornings to Martini and I will fancy that I am reading Petrarch; finally the evenings shall be given

---

[14] *Memorie,* vol. i, p. 128.
[15] Rob. Eitner, *Quellen-Lexikon,* vol. viii, p. 236.
[16] *Memorie,* vol. i, p. 129.
[17] Rob. Eitner, *Quellen-Lexikon,* vol. vii, p. 461.
[18] *Memorie,* vol. i, p. 130.

to Salieri and I will imagine that I am turning over the leaves of my Tasso."[19]

This time it was he who selected the subject of the new libretto for Mozart and his choice fell on the legend of Don Juan; for Martini he began to write *L' arbore di Diana;* and for Salieri, *Axur, re d' Ormus.*

It is amusing to read how the Poet began his work:

"A bottle of Tokay on my right, the inkstand before me, and a box of Spanish snuff on my left, I sat at my table for twelve consecutive hours. My landlady's daughter, a pretty girl of sixteen (for whom I wish I could have felt only a paternal affection) came to my room whenever I called for her, which was very often, especially when it seemed to me that I was losing my inspiration. Now and again she brought me a cake or a cup of coffee, and sometimes only her winsome little face, always gay and smiling, as if created to inspire poetical fancies and witty ideas."[20]

In the course of sixty-three days the libretti of *Don Giovanni* and *L' arbore di Diana* were completed, while only one-third of Salieri's opera remained unfinished.

Of the three works, the one which he esteemed the best was that written for Martini, the theme of which was the dissolution of monastic establishments by Joseph II, amusingly represented in an allegory in which Diana and her nymphs were outwitted by Cupid and Endymion.

It is more than probable that this plot was original; not so that of *Axur, re d' Ormus,* which, as he himself states,[21] was an Italian adaptation of the libretto *Tarare,* written by Beaumarchais and unsuccessfully

---

[19] *Memorie*, vol. i, p. 131.
[20] *Ibid.*
[21] *Ibid.*, vol. i, p. 130.

produced some time before by Salieri in Paris. As for *Don Giovanni,* hardly any doubt remains, especially after the already quoted study by Farinelli, that Da Ponte availed himself of other existing libretti, and in particular of that of Giovanni Bertati,[22] who was his successor, some years later, as "Poet to the Italian Theatre," and against whom he directed some caustic remarks in his *Memorie*.[23]

Yet this ought not entirely to deprive our Poet of the credit due to him, for, apart from the very selection of the subject which inspired Mozart's masterpiece, it is undeniable that the libretto has unusual qualities which ought to be taken into consideration.

"The common opinion," as one of Mozart's biographers very appropriately remarks, [24] "which considers the work of a librettist of small importance, is quite recent. At the time of Da Ponte, the relation between musician and poet was much closer than it is nowadays." Something similar to it can perhaps be found in the French comedy of the latter part of the last century where two authors coöperate in creating one play. The composition of the text of an opera was a specialty which required considerable study and gift, and which was held in great honor.

And, after what we know of Da Ponte's nature and adventurous life, is it not true that hardly an-

[22] Giovanni Bertati (1735-1815), born in Martellago, province of Treviso, started early to write for the stage and from 1771 to 1791 worked almost exclusively for the theatres of Venice. He succeeded Da Ponte in Vienna, after the dismissal of our Poet, but did not remain very long in his new position, and in 1794 returned to Venice, where he spent the rest of his life. He wrote no less than sixty libretti, some of which were set to music by leading composers.

[23] Vol. i, pp. 169-70.

[24] Ludwig Nohl, *The Life of Mozart* (transl. by Lady Wallace, London, 1877), p. 140.

other man could have been better qualified to treat the subject of *Don Giovanni?*

It was with keen insight, therefore, that Lamartine wrote, in his *Cours familier de Littérature*,[25] after reproducing the passage of the *Memorie* in which Lorenzo describes how he started to work on his play:

"C' est ainsi que Don Juan devait être écrit, par un aventurier, un amant, un poète, un homme de plaisir et de désordre inspiré du vin, de l'amour et de la gloire, entre les tentations de la débauche et le respect divin pour l'innocence, homme sans scrupule, mais non sans terreur des vengeances du ciel. D' Aponte [sic], à l'impénitence près, écrivait le drame de sa propre vie dans le drame de Don Juan."

Of the three plays written by our Poet, *L'arbore di Diana* was the first to be produced. It was given on October 1st, 1787,[26] on the occasion of the arrival in Vienna of the Archduchess Maria Theresa of Austria, bride of Prince Anthony of Saxony, as appears from the frontispiece of the libretto in its first edition.[27] It was received with favor both by the public and the Emperor, who appreciated Da Ponte's flattering tribute to his policies and sent him a gift of one hundred sequins.

Nearly a month later—to be precise, on the 29th of October—*Don Giovanni* was staged in Prague. That public, known for its passionate love for music.[28] and which the preceding year had received *Le nozze di Figaro* with unbounded enthusiasm, acclaimed the new opera a distinct triumph. Mozart, who came to direct it, was received with wild applause, which in-

[25] Tome v, p. 382.
[26] Rob. Eitner, *Quellen-Lexikon*, vol. vi, p. 350.
[27] F. Nicolini, Notes to the *Memorie*, vol. ii, p. 282.
[28] "Bohemia, where music was cultivated with enthusiasm, boasted just then of an exceptional scholastic system.

FACSIMILE OF THE PROGRAM OF THE FIRST PERFORM-
ANCE OF DON GIOVANNI

Observe in what small type the names of Da Ponte and Mozart appear in comparison with that of Guardassoni, the impresario.

creased in volume after each number and soon seemed to threaten to break all bounds of restraint.

Da Ponte, unfortunately, was not present. He had come to Prague but, as he informs us,[29] had been hurriedly recalled to Vienna, where Salieri, anxious to give his own opera, wanted him to finish the libretto for it.

From Mozart, we are told,[30] he received immediately after the first performance the following note:

"Our opera, *Don Giovanni*, was given last night before a very brilliant audience. The Princesses of Tuscany with their magnificent suites were present. It was received with such signs of approval that we could not have wished for more. Guardassoni [*the impresario*] came this morning to my room enthusiastically shouting: 'Long live Mozart! Long live Da Ponte! While these two live, impresari need not fear poverty!' Good-bye, my friend; prepare another opera for your
   MOZART."

It was not until six months later (May 7th, 1788) that the opera was performed in Vienna, where it met with an exceedingly cold reception. Salieri, whose

---

The teaching of music was obligatory even in the smallest village schools. The masters were required to have a tolerably wide knowledge of the arts and it was both the rule and the custom for each school-teacher to compose an annual mass to be performed by his pupils. Children who distinguished themselves at these little functions were noticed by the nobility and sent to superior schools where they received gratuitous education. All the best families had each a private chapel; their servants were expected to lend their services also as musicians." Victor Wilder, *Mozart* (trans. by L. Liebich, London), vol. ii, p. 280.

[29] *Memorie*, vol. i, p. 133.

[30] This note, which does not appear in any of the collections of Mozart's letters, was published by Da Ponte in one of his many polemics in America, and later by Bernardi (*L. Da Ponte*, p. 19) and Marchesan (*L. Da Ponte*, p. 111). F. Nicolini (Notes to the *Memorie*, vol. ii, p. 283) doubts its authenticity.

Axur, re d' Ormus—given for the first time on January 8th[31]—was enjoying immense popularity, endeavored to prevent its representation and it was only by the express command of the Emperor that *Don Giovanni* was given.

The interpretation, there is reason to suppose, was a very good one for the rôles were entrusted to first-rate artists: Benucci, who had created the part of Figaro, sang that of Leporello, Don Giovanni was the baritone Albertarelli, while the parts of Elvira and Anna were taken respectively by the Cavalieri and the composer's sister-in-law, Aloysia Lange. Yet, "How can I write it?" says Da Ponte in his *Memorie*,[32]

"*Don Giovanni* was a failure! All, save Mozart, believed that something was lacking. We added a little, we changed some songs, and it was given again. Again it failed!—'The opera is divine,' the Emperor asserted, 'it is perhaps superior to *Figaro,* but it is not food suited to the teeth of my Viennese.'—I related this to Mozart and he calmly replied: 'Let us give them time to chew it.'—He was right. I succeeded in arranging, by his advice, that the opera should be frequently repeated; at each performance the applause increased, and little by little the Viennese began to taste its beauty and to esteem *Don Giovanni* as one of the most beautiful operas ever produced for any stage."

About this time Italian opera in Vienna underwent a critical period. Lorenzo attributes this to the intrigues of certain singers,[33] but it is more likely that Joseph II felt obliged to withdraw his support owing

---

[31] Rob. Eitner, *Quellen-Lexikon*, vol. viii, p. 396.
[32] Vol. i, pp. 134-35.
[33] *Memorie*, vol. i, pp. 135-38.

to the depletion of the State's finances resulting from the campaign then being waged against the Turks.[34]

Da Ponte enlisted the support of private subscribers, and for some time managed to avert the necessity of discontinuing the performances. He wrote then for Salieri the libretto of *Il pastor fido,* taken from Guarini's drama. The opera was presented in the early part of 1789 and was indifferently received. Hardly a better success attended *La cifra,* written also for Salieri, and *Così fan tutte, o La scuola delle amanti,* which Mozart set to music.[35] On the contrary, *Il pasticcio,* a kind of "revue" in which he introduced the best selections of all the operas heard in Vienna during the last few seasons, seemed to arouse a certain interest. "It was," the author informs us,[36] "a rather witty and amusing criticism of the public, the impresari, the singers, the poets, the composers, and finally of myself."

The death of Joseph II, which occurred on February 20th, 1790, brought a sudden change in the fortunes of our Poet. Leopold II, who succeeded him, was quite a different type of man and he ascended the throne with the firm determination of pursuing a policy of restrictions and economy in contrast to his

---

[34] Evidence contradictory to his statement in the *Memorie* is found in a letter our Poet wrote on October 1st, 1788, to Antonio Michelini (Bernardi, *L. Da Ponte,* p. 225), in which the war against the Turks is given as the cause of the Emperor's decision.

[35] See *Memorie,* vol. i, p. 139. Mr. W. Littlefield, in an article published in *The New York Times* of April 2d, 1922, claims that the libretto of *Così fan tutte* was not written by Da Ponte. His contention, based on several arguments, but mainly on the assumed fact that not a word in the *Memorie* refers to this opera, was disproved point by point by the present writer in an article which appeared in *The New York Times* of April 23d. Mr. H. E. Krehbiel also took issue with Mr. Littlefield in the columns of the *New York Tribune.* See Bibliography, Nos. 97-101.

[36] *Memorie,* vol. i, p. 139.

late brother's prodigality. In addition to this unfavorable attitude of the sovereign, other events concurred to undermine, despite his efforts to maintain his former prestige, the position held by Da Ponte; and, as will soon be seen, it was again a woman to whom he owed his downfall.

Extremely busy with state affairs, Leopold ignored a *canzone* which Lorenzo wrote soon after his accession to the throne, mourning the death of Joseph and lauding in flattering hyperboles his successor. For a time, it seems, the old order of things remained unchanged, and when, towards the end of that year, Ferdinand IV of Naples came to Vienna, accompanied by his Queen and his two daughters, Princesses Maria Theresa and Maria Louise, brides respectively of the future Emperor Francis and of his brother Ferdinand, Lorenzo was asked to compose something in honor of the illustrious guests. He wrote then a *cantata* entitled *Flora e Minerva,* which was set to music by Joseph Weigl, [37] and presented with great success, on January 17th, 1791,[38] before the assembled court.

Another *cantata,* probably the one entitled *I voti della nazione napoletana,* for which Francesco Piticchio composed the music and which was given a month or so later, was written by Lorenzo at the request of the Neapolitan ambassador, Marquis Del Gallo. It was

[37] Joseph Weigl (1766-1846), born in Eisenstadt, studied music under Albrechtsberger and Salieri and at a very early age showed exceptional talent for his art. His first opera, *Die unnütze Vorsicht* (1782) made him widely known, and when six years later he produced *Il pazzo per forza* his reputation was established. He had composed about 30 operas up to 1825, in which year he succeeded Salieri as court conductor. His time henceforth was almost entirely devoted to masses, offertories and graduals.

[38] The date appears on the frontispiece of the original score. Nicolini, Notes to the *Memorie*, vol. ii, p. 285.

the last production of our Poet in Vienna, for the storm which had been gathering for some time burst upon him, resulting in his dismissal.

Little has been said about the love adventures of Lorenzo during his stay in the Austrian capital,— mainly for the reason that little is known in regard to this. Yet we should be innocent-minded to suppose that the devil had become a hermit, especially if we take into account the temptations of the theatrical environment in which our abbé moved. At any rate, after protesting that for the first seven years of his poetical career in Vienna he had resisted the allurements of the stage beauties, he admits[39] that he fell precipitately in love with Adriana Gabrielli-Del Bene, a singer widely known in the musical world of that time under the name of "Ferrarese."

According to his confession, the relation between them was not of recent date in 1791, and it would not be surprising if the matter had caused a great deal of gossip. The trouble started when Da Ponte, trying at all costs to secure a new contract for his protégée antagonized the other singers to such an extent that they appealed to the Emperor, and, as it seems,[40] even to the Empress, accusing him of underhanded intrigues and favoritism. As a result he was dismissed and ordered to leave Vienna.

Deciding to leave no stone unturned in his effort to rehabilitate himself, he retired then to the neighboring village of Moedling,[41] wherefrom he tried in vain by several means to obtain an audience with the sovereign. In the *Memorie*[42] it is stated that at this time

[39] *Memorie*, vol. i, pp. 138-40.
[40] *Ibid.*, vol. i, p. 145.
[41] Nicolini, Notes to the *Memorie*, vol. ii, p. 287.
[42] Vol. i, p. 147.

Martini wrote him from St. Petersburg asking him to come there, and that he declined the invitation; but it is much more likely that it was he who solicited an appointment at the court of Russia from the Spanish composer and received no encouragement, for it appears inconceivable that, his circumstances being what they were, he could have refused such an offer, had it been made.

He turned then to Mozart with the peculiar proposition that they should go together to London and try their luck there; but Mozart, as he states,[43] being busy at that time with his *Magic Flute,* asked for six months time before giving a definite answer. That this is true, there is no reason to doubt, in view of a letter declining to entertain the project, written in the autumn of that year by the great composer to our Poet, who was then in Trieste. This letter (which has been passed over unnoticed by all of Da Ponte's biographers, probably on account of the fact that in the collections of Mozart's letters it is assigned "to an unknown recipient," though undoubtedly it was addressed to Lorenzo) is in Italian. It bears the date "Vienna, September, 1791," and its contents show that it was written at the time when the composer, altogether absorbed in his last work (the *Requiem Mass*), was suffering from those strange hallucinations that preceded his premature death.

"My dear Sir," he writes, "I should like to take your advice, but how can I? My spirit is broken and I cannot divert my eyes from the vision of that stranger. I see him continually before me; he entreats and urges me, and impatiently asks for my work. I continue to compose because that fatigues me less than resting. Anyhow, I have nothing more to fear. I

---

[43] *Memorie,* vol. i, p. 147.

GLORY AND DOWNFALL

know well, from what I am experiencing, that my hour is near, that I am on the boundary line of life and death: I shall die without having known any of the delights my talent would have brought me. And yet life is so full of beauty, and just at present my career shows auspicious prospects! Alas! one cannot alter one's own destiny. Nobody on earth is master of his fate, and I must be resigned; it will be as Providence decrees. For myself I must complete my funeral hymn and I would not like to leave my work unfinished."[44]

Disappointed also in this, Da Ponte made an effort to obtain through the good offices of his old protectors, Memmo, Zaguri and Da Lezze, a pardon from the Venetian government, so as to be permitted to return to his native country. Here again he was unsuccessful,[45] and the "Ferrarese," who went to Venice with her husband presumably to intercede also for him, seems to have made matters still worse.[46]

What occurred after Da Ponte saw that, despite all his efforts, no results were attained in his favor and that the Emperor refused to see him, we can only

[44] Aff.mo Signore, Vorrei seguire il vostro consiglio, ma come riuscirvi? Ho il capo frastornato, conto [campo?] a forza, e non posso levarmi dagli occhi l' immagine di questo incognito. Lo vedo di continuo; esso mi prega, mi sollecita, ed impaziente mi chiede il lavoro. Continuo, perchè il comporre mi stanca meno del riposo. Altronde non ho più da tremere [sic]. Lo sento a quel che provo, che l' ora suona; sono in procinto di spirare; ho finito prima di avar [sic] goduto del mio talento. La vita era pur sì bella, la carriera s' appriva [sic] sotto auspici tanto fortunati, ma non si può cangiare il proprio destino. Nessuno misura i propri giorni, bisogna rassegnarsi, sarà quel che piacerà alla provvidenza, termino, ecco il mio canto funebre non devo lasciarlo imperfetto. Mozart.—*Die Briefe W. A. Mozarts*, vol. ii, p. 350.

[45] See in this regard the letters dated June 11th, 1791, July 13th of the same year and April 21st, 1792, from Pietro Zaguri to Casanova. Molmenti, *Cart. Casan.*, vol. ii, pp. 141, 149 and 177.

[46] *Memorie*, vol. i, p. 162. The fact that the "Ferrarese" went to Venice for the reason stated, is mentioned also in a

divine, since no clue is given in his *Memorie*. It may be surmised that, in a peevish mood, he must have said or written something abusive which caused offense to some personage of high rank, for one night he was taken from his bed by the police, brought to Vienna and there allowed twenty-four hours to quit the capital and its environs.

He went thereupon to Trieste, where, as we have seen, he later received from Mozart the letter above quoted. The date at which he reached that city must have been about the end of June or the beginning of July, for in a letter from Zaguri to Casanova, dated July 13th, 1791, there is mention of the Poet's being there.[47]

Curiously enough, it is only at this point in the *Memorie* that we learn he was not unaccompanied. He had with him, in fact, and under his charge, on his arrival in Trieste, a woman—"who," to use his own words, "had been a constant friend of mine for ten years, and who had followed me in my misfortune," —together with two of his half-brothers, probably Agostino and Paolo.[48]

His main object in coming to that city was to obtain an audience with Leopold II, who, having made a journey through Italy, was expected to spend a few days there on his way back to Vienna. Accordingly, Lorenzo went at once to call on the governor, Count

---

letter written by Da Ponte to Casanova, from Vienna, on June 18th, 1791. Molmenti, *Cart. Casan.*, vol. i, pp. 264-65. On the other hand, Zaguri wrote to the old Venetian adventurer: "He was crazy about the Ferrarese; said he had lost everything for her, but she left him and wrote to him no more." *Ibid.*, vol. ii, p. 159.

[47] Molmenti, *Cart. Casan.*, vol. ii, p. 149.

[48] *Memorie*, vol. i, p. 160. Who this woman was and what became of her, remains a mystery.

W. A. MOZART

FROM AN UNFINISHED PORTRAIT BY J. LANGE, AT THE MOZART-
MUSEUM IN SALZBURG.

Brigido (1729-1811), and, having explained his case, succeeded in securing a promise of assistance.

A few days later the audience was obtained, but not without difficulty. It seems that the Emperor, having recognized the abbé in a theatre, turned to Baron Pittoni, commissioner of police, with the remark that the man was a scoundrel who should not be tolerated and that by his order he had been expelled from the capital. Whereupon Governor Brigido took it upon himself to inform His Majesty that the poet had come to Trieste for the express purpose of begging an audience with him, in order to point out that he had been the victim of an injustice. Leopold refused to see him and repeated his first order, but the next day he changed his mind: Da Ponte was summoned to the royal presence and allowed to present his defense.[49]

Lorenzo's version of the lengthy interview is given almost word for word in the *Memorie*.[50] But although he emphatically states that what he relates is the perfect truth, not too much faith can be accorded him. He would have us believe that the Emperor, fully convinced of his innocence, gave him some vague promise of rehabilitation,—which he afterwards did not keep; but if this was the case, it is hard to understand why his request to be permitted to return to Vienna was denied. That the money offered him by Leopold was nobly refused, also seems improbable. What he says, however, about his accusations against those "who had ruined him,"—accusations which the Emperor required him to commit to writing,—is more likely, and it is

---

[49] These details are taken from a letter written by Baron Pittoni to Giacomo Casanova on September 6th, 1791. See Molmenti, *Cart. Casan.*, vol. i, p. 233.
[50] Vol. i, pp. 152-59.

conceivable that it was precisely as a reward for this sort of espionage that he was permitted to remain in Trieste.[51]

There he lived for some time on the savings he had brought with him from Vienna; but within a short time he and those dependent upon him were reduced to a bare subsistence and we are informed that one by one he parted with the contents of his wardrobe in order to provide for daily needs.

For three months he thus struggled against adversity. Meanwhile an operatic troupe had arrived in Trieste and they were on the eve of producing *L' ape musicale* (another title for his *Il pasticcio*), when he was asked to assist the impresario in its performance; this relieved, at least temporarily, his financial embarrassment. A little later another opportunity presented itself, when a tragedy, *Il Mezenzio,* the first two acts of which had been written by his brother Luigi and which he completed, was staged by a dramatic company.[52]

It was at that time—towards the end of 1791— that Da Ponte became acquainted with the family of John Grahl, a merchant, native of Dresden, who had lived for many years in England and only shortly before Lorenzo's arrival in Trieste had settled in that city.[53] Received as a friend by these strangers, who

[51] Nicolini, Notes to the *Memorie*, vol. ii, p. 288.

[52] No doubt exists that this was the play alluded to in the *Memorie*, for the present writer found in the New York Public Library a copy of the tragedy, bearing the following title: *Il Mezenzio, tragedia originale di Lorenzo Da Ponte, rappresentata nel Ces. Reg. Teatro di Trieste, per la prima volta, l' autunno dell' anno* 1791. *Nuova Jorka, Joseph Desmones, Stampatore,* 1834.

[53] In a passage of the *Memorie* (vol. i, p. 230) Nancy Grahl, some time after her marriage to Da Ponte, in answer to a question as to her ability to speak various languages, is reported as having said: "I am an English woman, sir.

were glad perhaps to have found somebody who took an interest in them, Da Ponte soon knew how to win their affection, attracted as he was by the extraordinary beauty and youthful charms of the merchant's youngest daughter, Nancy.[54]

It is clearly stated in the *Memorie* that she at first felt no special inclination towards him,—a fact which is not surprising since she was twenty years younger than he. But the circumstance that they met almost daily, for she began to take Italian lessons from him, giving French in exchange, little by little engendered warmer feelings in her, and this eventually determined her destiny.

When, early in March, the news reached Trieste that Leopold II had passed away,[55] Lorenzo, who meanwhile had tried by several means to have the Emperor reminded of his "promises," decided that the best thing for him to do would be to go to Vienna and press his case personally before the new sovereign. From the Bishop of Trieste, to whom he first turned for assistance, he received only the meagre consolation that he would pray to God for his case; but Governor Brigido, to whom he next addressed himself,

---

I speak French because I have been for some time in France; German, as my father was born in Dresden; Dutch, since I have lived also in Holland; and Italian, for the reason that it is the language of my husband."

[54] Her full name, it seems, was Anna Celestine Ernestine. See Bibliography, I, A, 9.

[55] Leopold died March 1st, 1792. Lorenzo states that he went to Vienna by the permission and through the help of the governor of Trieste, and that only when he had reached that city did the Emperor's death become known. But it is hardly conceivable that the governor would have disregarded the sovereign's orders while the latter was still alive, and therefore we are justified in assuming that Leopold had already died when our Poet started on his journey. This opinion is also held by Nicolini (Notes to the *Memorie*, vol. ii, p. 290).

showed more willingness to help him: he furnished him with a permission to leave for the capital and gave him twenty-five sequins for his traveling expenses.

In Vienna, singularly enough, it was Casti, whose ambition to become a Caesarean Poet had finally been realized, who undertook his defense. At his suggestion and in his company, Da Ponte went to see Count Saur, head of the police, and there Casti was so successful in pleading his cause that he aroused the sympathy of that official and induced him to use his influence in behalf of Lorenzo. While the audience which Da Ponte had hoped to get was not granted, he obtained from the Emperor a pecuniary bonus of one hundred sovereigns, and permission to remain in the capital as long as he chose.[56]

He remained, however, only three weeks and then returned to Trieste, planning this time to try his luck at the court of France, where he hoped to obtain the protection of Marie Antoinette, an admirer—as the late Emperor Joseph had told him—of his *Una cosa rara*.[57]

[56] In a letter dated March 28th, 1792, Count de Collalto wrote to Casanova:

"Madame Ferrarese has stopped over in Vienna for a few days on her way to Warsaw, where she has been engaged for that theatre. Also Abbé Da Ponte has been seen here, but, as far as I know, her husband did not allow him to come to their house. They say that the poet has begged His Majesty for many things, among which are two as to which I do not know whether or not they accord with the facts: 1st, to be reinstated in his lost position; 2d, to be given some money, it being claimed that the late Emperor had promised to provide for him and had ordered him to remain in Trieste meanwhile, that relying on these words he had not attempted to procure other employment, and that it would only be fair to give him some financial assistance." Molmenti, *Cart. Casan.*, vol. i, pp. 66-67.

[57] *Memorie*, vol. i, p. 166.

It is interesting to read in his autobiography how it happened that, before embarking on this new venture, he wooed and won the fair Nancy. At the beginning of his relations with the Grahl family, we are told, he had tried to arrange an advantageous marriage between the young lady and an Italian gentleman residing in Vienna. There had been an exchange of portraits and matters had reached almost the point of an engagement, when the plan was suddenly discarded by the girl's father, who probably had noticed with satisfaction the growing attachment between Nancy and Lorenzo.

"I was sitting beside her, one evening," he writes,[58] "when her brother came in with a letter for me. I recognized the handwriting, opened the letter with a trembling hand and a sinking heart, and read aloud: 'My dear friend,—the young woman, if she resembles her picture, is very beautiful; the information I have received from all my friends as to her character, habits and manners, could not be more pleasing. But, as I understand that her father is quite wealthy, I would like to inquire, though I myself am well-to-do, what dowry he intends to give his daughter as a protection for her future children.'

"I had scarcely finished reading, when Mr. Grahl snatched the paper out of my hand, tore it to pieces and threw them into the fire, exclaiming in anger these words: 'So it is my money, not my daughter, that Signor Galliano wishes to marry!' (Galliano was the gentleman's name.) He remained silent for a few moments, paced up and down the room three or four times, and then, turning abruptly to me: 'Da Ponte,' he said, 'do you want her?'—'Whom?' asked I smiling. 'My daughter,' he replied. And as I kept on smiling, he turned to the girl: 'And you, Nancy, what do you say about it? Do you want him?' She lowered her eyes, smiled, raised them again, looked at me with

[58] *Memorie*, vol. i, p. 164.

sweet modesty; and her father, who saw in our smiles and silence what was in our hearts, joined our hands together, and to me he said: 'Nancy is yours;' to her: 'Da Ponte is yours.' Her mother, brother, and sister-in-law applauded this improvised scene; but my joy, and I believe hers also, was so deep in that moment, that our emotion rendered us speechless for the rest of the evening."

Whether, after this, they were married, as Lorenzo seems to intimate,[59] or whether they simply eloped, as Baron Pittoni indicates in a letter he wrote to Giacomo Casanova,[60] is a matter of conjecture. At any rate, on August 12th, 1792, they started from Trieste, partners for life, with the intention of establishing themselves in Paris.

[59] "After social ceremonies and formalities, she was given to me by her parents." *Memorie*, vol. i, p. 176.
[60] "Da Ponte left Trieste with the self-styled daughter of an English merchant called Kral, who shortly after went bankrupt and also fled; and we have been informed that all were apprehended in Ostend." Molmenti. *Cart. Casan.*, vol. i, p. 237.

CHAPTER V

DA PONTE'S LONDON CAREER

On leaving Trieste on their long journey, all the worldly possessions of Lorenzo and Nancy consisted of about six hundred florins, the horse and carriage in which they were traveling, and the parting gift of one hundred florins in gold which Nancy had received from her mother,—and which unfortunately was lost while they were on their way to Prague.[1]

Arriving in that city, Da Ponte, remembering that Casanova, then librarian of the Count of Waldstein in the nearby Dux, owed him some money, decided to surprise him with a visit. Both he and Nancy were received with great cordiality by the old adventurer, but the hope they had entertained proved vain, for our Poet found his friend in such straightened circumstances that he did not even mention the real motive of their trip. Yet they remained as his guests for three or four days, and when finally they started for Dresden, Casanova, we are told, gave Lorenzo the following advice, which, as the latter himself admits, might have saved him a good deal of trouble had he strictly adhered to it: "If you are seeking luck, my dear Da Ponte, do not go to Paris, go to London;

[1] The occurrence is related with curious details in the *Memorie* (vol. i, pp. 176-77). The lost sum, however, was recovered several months later, reaching the couple in a moment of great need. A peasant had found it, had handed it to the parish priest of the next village, and the latter, knowing the case and being informed of the owners' itinerary, forwarded it to them.

once there never enter the Italian Café and never sign your name."[2]

Though hardly of any importance in itself, the meeting of the two adventurers in Dux has seemed worth relating in consideration of the fact that it led to an active correspondence between them. Da Ponte's letters to Casanova, recently published by Molmenti[3] —which, except for one, are all subsequent to this visit —are richer in details and give us more trustworthy information than the *Memorie* in regard to this period of his life.

In Dresden, where they arrived by stage-coach, for their own carriage had broken down near Teplitz and had there been sold together with the horse, our couple found themselves warmly received by Lorenzo's old friends, Father Huber and Caterino Mazzolà.

As it appears from the above-mentioned correspondence, they remained in that city from the 16th to the 27th of September, 1792, during which time our reckless Poet seems to have squandered in amusements a great part of his money, relying on a hoped-for remittance from Trieste which Nancy had solicited from her parents. We are told also that he had planned to see Count Marcolini, who he had hoped could do something for him, but that Mazzolà—and his motive can easily be understood—dissuaded him from so doing.[4]

When, a few days later, Lorenzo and Nancy had reached Spires, they learned to their dismay that the French sovereigns had been imprisoned and the revolutionary army had advanced on German territory as far as Mayence. The whole plan of their journey had

---

[2] *Memorie*, vol. i, p. 178.
[3] *Cart. Casan.*, vol. i, pp. 260-316.
[4] Molmenti, *Cart. Casan.*, vol. i, p. 268.

GIACOMO CASANOVA

FROM A PORTRAIT BY FRANCESCO CASANOVA, DACHOFF COLLECTION, PETROGRAD.

then to be revised and, taking Casanova's advice, they started for London by way of Holland. On their arrival in the English metropolis, their resources were almost exhausted: all they had was a few louis, a gold watch, and a ring which was sold for six guineas. They stopped at first with one of Nancy's sisters, but, as she and her husband were "neither rich nor generous,"[5] the couple sought other quarters in a little furnished room, where it was not long before they found themselves in absolute poverty.

The managers of the Drury Lane Theatre in Haymarket were at that time two of Da Ponte's old acquaintances, Michael Kelly and the composer Storace; and Lorenzo, with his heart full of hopes, turned to them asking for the position of poet to the theatre,— a post left vacant by the recent death of a certain Antonioli.[6] Having been told that the promise of an engagement had already been made to Carlo Francesco Badini, a librettist who had previously occupied the same position, he proposed that at least he be engaged to furnish two libretti a year.

While these negotiations were pending, Lorenzo found a sympathic friend in the musician Pietro Dal Pozzo, who not only assisted him financially but introduced him to the famous prima donna, Mara,[7]

[5] *Memorie*, vol. i, p. 186.
[6] For this and other details concerning Da Ponte's first stay in London, see his letters to Casanova dated Jan. 19th, March 1st, April 2nd and May 10th, 1793. Molmenti, *Cart. Casan.*, vol. i, pp. 273-90.
[7] Gertrude Elizabeth Schmoelling Mara (1749-1833) was one of the greatest singers of the latter part of the XVIII century. Born in Cassel, Germany, as a child she was a violin prodigy and her father presented her in Vienna and London. In that city she took singing lessons from Paradisi, showing such exceptional talents that henceforth she devoted herself entirely to the vocal art. After singing in Leipzig and Dresden, she was engaged in 1771 by the Berlin Court

who had recently arrived in London and who took such a lively interest in our Poet as to request him to write a libretto for her. It did not take him long to comply with her wish: an adaptation from his tragedy *Il Mezenzio* satisfied the singer and brought him twenty-five guineas.

When in December Badini was finally appointed to the position Lorenzo had coveted, and the latter saw that his second proposition also had been ignored, he decided to avenge himself "nobly" by founding a libellous newspaper which was to be published immediately following each operatic production, "in order," as he explained to his friend Casanova, to whom he also sent a prospectus, "to have these gentlemen understand that they have made a big mistake in treating me that way." He had even decided on the title, which was to be *La bilancia musicale,* when lack of subscriptions made him abandon his idea.

Seeing this plan frustrated, Da Ponte endeavored to obtain through the influence of some high personages[8] that which had been denied him by Kelly and Storace, and, hoping to enhance his reputation thereby, he published in February 1793 a pamphlet with the title of *Il tributo del core,* containing a long *canzone,* and an aria with chorus, and twelve sonnets, all dealing with the sad fate of Louis XVI.[9] Badini, aware

---

Opera. In Berlin she married the violincellist Mara. She went to Vienna in 1780 and two years later to Paris, where she ruled supreme up to the Reign of Terror, when she fled to London. In her old age she was a singing teacher in Russia. She died in Reval in great poverty.

[8] He mentions in this regard the Duke of Bedford and the Marquis of Salisbury.

[9] A copy of this pamphlet, now a bibliographical rarity, was discovered among Casanova's papers by Aldo Ravà. See his article *Un' operetta sconosciuta sulla morte di Luigi XVI,* in *Marzocco,* June 25th, 1911.

of the intrigues of our Poet, took this occasion to belittle him by publishing a scurrilous parody on his verses, *Il tributo della coglionatura*. Lorenzo, of course, was not the kind of a man to ignore this attack; he retaliated, and there ensued a battle of violent invectives, which for some months must have been the delight of London theatre-goers.

All this, however, did not solve the problem of existence for him and his young wife, soon to become a mother. So he followed new advice given to him by Casanova and, leaving Nancy with her sister, set out in search of better luck for Brussels, where he arrived on the 10th of July. His purpose in going there was to promote the establishment of an Italian theatre. At first it seemed as though the project might prove a success, inasmuch as the auspices under which it was to be launched were most favorable. Our Poet asserts that he was able to gain the confidence and coöperation of such prominent families as those of Aremberg, Metternich, Ligne and Rohan. The number of subscribers increased from day to day, encouraged by which he wrote to Nancy to join him.

She came, but the project formed by Da Ponte did not materialize owing to the excessive demands made by some of the singers, and the couple soon left for Holland with the intention of renewing their efforts there. At the Hague, however, the result was hardly better, for after success in securing a large number of subscribers for an opera scheduled to be given alternately in the Hague and in Amsterdam, the disastrous news of the complete defeat of the English near Dunkirk arrived to upset everything. Fear of the victorious French army's approach spread consternation throughout the country and our Poet found himself of a sudden deprived of all support.

He and Nancy passed then through a period of distressing privation. In vain he appealed to Casanova and the latter's protector, the Count of Waldstein, to whom he even addressed some stanzas in the hope of softening his heart.[10] "Our breakfast," he writes in recalling those hard days,[11] "consisted of bread, bread was our dinner, and sometimes we had not even bread for supper, but tears."

How long this painful situation lasted we are not told; probably only a few days. When things seemed at the worst and even their landlord had requested them to vacate their room, a letter came from London in which Nancy's sister wrote that Badini had been dismissed from his position by the impresario of the Drury Lane Theatre, William Taylor, and that he, Da Ponte, had been selected to fill his place. Thus our Poet's ambition was finally crowned and moreover it seemed as if he could look towards a future free from financial difficulties.

That his pathway, however, was not going to be strewn with roses, soon became apparent on his return to London in the last days of December 1793. Besides having to contend with the impresario, whose typical Anglo-Saxon reserve was an enigma to him and repellent to his temperamental nature,[12] he had

[10] They were enclosed in a letter to Casanova dated October 13th, 1793. Molmenti, *Cart. Casan.*, vol. i, pp. 298-304.

[11] *Memorie*, vol. i, p. 189.

[12] This is the account he gives of his first interview, if we may call it so, with Taylor:

"He was writing at a desk when his friend Federici brought me into his office. He had his back turned towards the door and faced the window.—'Here is Mr. Da Ponte,' said Federici. The impresario continued to write without turning.—'Mr. Taylor, here is the poet,' Federici added a little louder. At this the impresario turned, nodded and again resumed his writing. I remained in the room five minutes, after which Signor Federici made me understand with signs

to face the resentful enmity of Badini and to use all his diplomatic skill in dealing with the artists of the theatre, whose cabals and mutual jealousies had no limit.

Among the singers engaged for the opera were the famous prime donne Banti[13] and Morichelli,[14] whom our poet describes as "equals in their vices, passions and perfidy," and of whom in his *Memorie* he gives a vivid, though certainly not flattering picture.[15] He was commissioned to write a libretto for each of them: one for Banti, the music of which was to be composed by Francesco Bianchi;[16] the other for Mori-

---

to depart quietly. Frankly it did not seem an auspicious beginning to me, who had for ten years been the poet of Joseph II, a prince who was the true model of affability, goodness and courtesy." *Memorie*, vol. i, p. 193.

[13] Brigida Giorgi Banti (1759-1806) had a most peculiar career as a prima donna. Born in Crema, Lombardy, in the poorest surroundings, she began at a very early age as a *cantante di piazza*, or street singer. At the age of 19 she started for Paris, earning her way by singing in cafés and inns. Discovered in a boulevard café by the operatic manager Des Vismes, she soon after appeared in grand opera charming everybody with the qualities and phenomenal range of her voice. Devoid of any education and a most rebellious pupil, she relied wholly on her ear and intuitive feeling for music, in her singing. She sang for several years in London, appeared also in Italy, and died at the age of 47 in Bologna.

[14] Anna Bosello Morichelli (1760-?), a native of Reggio Emilia, had also a good voice. Trained by Guadagni, she sang for the first time in Parma (1779), then appeared in Venice and Milan; was in Vienna during the season 1781-82, and, after other performances in Italy, was engaged by Viotti for the *Théâtre de Monsieur* in Paris. In London she sang from 1792 to 1794, after which she returned to Italy and retired from the stage.

[15] *Memorie*, vol. i, pp. 194-5.

[16] Francesco Bianchi (1752-1810), of Cremona, started his career as a pianist. In 1775 he was appointed *maestro di cembalo* to the Italian Opera in Paris; there he composed his first opera, *La réduction de Paris*. When in 1780 his *Castore e Polluce* was given in Florence, his reputation was made and he started on his prolific production of operas, 50 in number.

chelli, which was to be entrusted to the composer Martini, who at Da Ponte's invitation had come to London from Russia and was now living with him.

Of the two works, *La capricciosa corretta* seemed to proceed faster owing to the fact that Martini was at hand, inspiring the Poet with his music, which he composed with surprising facility, scene after scene, almost as rapidly as the words were handed to him. The opera was almost completed after a few months and found full of charms by the few who were privileged to hear some of its passages, while of *Merope* only the first act had been delivered to Bianchi, in spite of Banti's persistent pressure.

It is easy to imagine in what a temper she complained to the impresario—with whom it seems she was on very familiar terms—when she heard praises of the opera written for her rival. Da Ponte was severely taken to task for his neglect and, as a result, *Merope's* second act was finished by him within twenty-four hours, according at least to his statement in the *Memorie*.[17] This, however, did not settle the imbroglio, for now it was the composer who, offended, was not disposed to write the music. So *Merope* was shelved[18] and, instead, it was arranged to present as a new opera *Aci e Galatea,* composed by the same Bianchi years before. This proved a failure.

La capricciosa corretta, on the contrary, given shortly after, was received by the London public with such marked favor, despite all intrigues, that Da

---

In 1793 he went to London, where he remained up to 1800, engaged by the Drury Lane Theatre. Ten years later he committed suicide.

[17] Vol. i, p. 197.

[18] Later Bianchi composed the music for it, and it was produced in 1799. Eitner, *Quellen-Lexikon*, vol. ii, p. 29.

Ponte immediately started to write another libretto for Martini. This was *L' isola del piacere,* which, however, obtained a less enthusiastic success. Its lukewarm reception is attributed by Lorenzo to the strained relations which he says existed between him and the composer while the second act was being written. Their break, as related in the *Memorie,*[19] originated as follows: the composer had seduced a maid in Lorenzo's home and being reproached by the jealous Morichelli, with whom he was on terms of intimacy, had exculpated himself by throwing the responsibility on Da Ponte; informed of this, our Poet had bitterly resented the false accusation and, after an unpleasant scene, Martini had taken other quarters.

There is no means of ascertaining when the two operas were performed for the first time. Kelly, in his *Reminiscences,* gives no clue, and it is curious, to say the least, that he does not even mention our Poet in connection with what was going on at the Drury Lane Theatre. Fortunately, a letter which Da Ponte wrote to Casanova on August 25th, 1795[20] helps us to fix at least approximately the time in which the two productions were given. In it, besides relating with bitter expressions the story of his break with the Spanish composer, he states that he had written for him two libretti. It will then not be far from the truth to assert that *La capricciosa corretta* must have been produced in 1794, while *L' isola del piacere* probably was given at the beginning of 1795.

But were these the only two operas for which Lorenzo wrote libretti during the first two years of his engagement at the Drury Lane Theatre?

[19] Vol. i, pp. 198-99.
[20] Molmenti, *Cart. Casan.,* vol. i, pp. 312-16. This is the last of Da Ponte's letters to his old friend in Dux.

Two pamphlets, referred to by H. E. Krehbiel in his article on our Poet,[21] and which the present writer had an opportunity to examine in the library of the New York Historical Society, show that another production not mentioned in the *Memorie* must be ascribed to him, *La scuola de' martitati,*—unless indeed this be another title for one of the above-mentioned operas.[22]

The first of these pamphlets, written anonymously and purporting to have been printed in Lisbon, has the following title: "A Short Notice on the Opera Buffa by the title *La scuola de' maritati,* written by the celebrated Lorenzo Daponte [*sic*], who after having been Jew, Christian, priest and poet in Italy and Germany, found himself to be a layman, husband and ass in London." It is a venomous libel, in which the most repulsive and obscene language is employed. From certain passages it appears that it was written two years after Da Ponte's arrival in London, that is in 1795.

Who its author was would have been easy to guess, even if the next pamphlet, anonymous also but undoubtedly written by Lorenzo, had not clearly pointed in both its title and contents to Carlo Francesco Badini.[23] It goes without saying that the answer is at least as violent as the attack.

[21] *Da Ponte in New York*, published for the first time in the *New York Tribune*, August 28th, 1887, then in his *Review of New York Musical Season 1889-90*, finally in his *Music and Manners in the Classical Period.* New York, Scribner, 1899.

[22] Or possibly, on account of the resemblance of the titles, it may have been *Cosi fan tutte o La scuola delle amanti*, which Da Ponte wrote in Vienna for Mozart.

[23] The title of Da Ponte's pamphlet says it is an answer to a libel by "Carlo Francesco . . . . . ." In the text this illuminating phrase is found: "We have wished to answer thus, *pour badiner*," and the French expression is further elucidated by the following note: "The grammarians say that the

The letter to Casanova, a part of which was quoted above, furnishes some interesting information about Lorenzo's family life, a point on which his biography, otherwise so replete with useless details, is singularly obscure. After telling his friend that his salary had been reduced, he says: "To offset this deficit, I have rented from the impresario the café of the theatre and shall install my Nancy as supervisor: if things go well, we can earn about one hundred pounds, which would make up for the other loss." And a few lines below he adds: "Nancy asks to be remembered to you and wishes to know whether you are willing that her second child should be baptized with your name."

This is the first mention made of Da Ponte's children; as will later be seen, the first two were girls.

Meanwhile his relations with Taylor and Banti seem to have become more cordial,—which is hardly to be wondered at when we read in his autobiography that, at their request, forgetting the advice given him by Casanova, he had endorsed a considerable number of notes for Taylor, who, leading a very dissolute life, was always in need of money.[24]

That he, who already in Vienna and in Holland had had dealings with usurers,[25] should have lent his name as innocently and disinterestedly as he wishes us to believe, is almost incredible. And when he later tells how Banti had become infatuated with him even to the point of wanting him to spend a summer in her villa, and adds that he resisted her allurements,

---

root of this verb is Badin."—Mr. Krehbiel seems to have mistaken Francesco for a surname. See his note on p. 165 in *Music and Manners*.

[24] *Memorie*, vol. i, pp. 203-6.

[25] See in this regard his letters to Casanova from Belgium and Holland. Molmenti, *Cart. Casan.*, vol. i, 290-312.

we simply cannot picture him acting the part of Joseph to Potiphar's wife. It is more likely that, wholly under her influence, and perhaps also deriving an immediate benefit by it, he endorsed Taylor's note, —for it was Taylor who was paying her bills. Nor must we forget that probably he had not even the slightest suspicion that the impresario would fail to honor his own signature.

From 1795 to 1798 Da Ponte's production for the Drury Lane Theatre seems to have been limited to a *cantata* on the occasion of the wedding of the Prince of Wales (George IV) with Elizabeth of Brunswick; *Evelina,* a play in three acts, set to music by Sacchini and Rey, and *Semira e Azor,* the music of which had been previously composed by Grétry.[26] The two latter were merely translations from the French.

It was during the fall of 1798 that Taylor asked Da Ponte whether he would like to go to Italy for the purpose of engaging a good prima donna and a tenor of reputation, allowing him one hundred guineas for traveling expenses. Naturally, he accepted the proposition enthusiastically, especially inasmuch as after the fall of the Venetian Republic his banishment had become ineffective. And thus, after nineteen years of exile, he had a chance of seeing his family and his native town once more.

Another errand, it seems, was entrusted to him:

[26] André Ernest Modeste Grétry (1741-1813) was born in Liége, where he started as a choir boy. In 1759 he was sent to Italy to study music, but proved a very poor student. He left Rome in 1767 with the singular idea of going to Geneva to ask for a libretto from Voltaire. All he received was the advice to go to Paris. In the French capital he made himself known as a composer of a certain ability, though overshadowed by the fame of Méhul and Cherubini. His operas, about 50, show but a superficial knowledge of the theory of music and the science of harmony.

that of bringing from Italy Banti's little son.[27] He took his wife along; on October 10th they landed in Hamburg, and on the 2d of November they reached Castelfranco, a charming little town not far from Ceneda. There, we are told, he left Nancy while he journeyed alone to his home town, telling her to meet him two days after in the nearby Treviso.

"Nous ne connaissons dans aucune langue," says Lamartine,[28] referring to the pages of the *Memorie* in which our Poet relates his return to the paternal roof, "des scènes domestiques qui remuent plus doucement et plus profondément les fibres de famille." And indeed these are the most sincere and touching passages in Lorenzo's autobiography.

He was going to find at Ceneda his almost octogenarian father, three half-brothers, seven half-sisters, their children, brothers-in-law, sisters-in-law, old friends and school-fellows, all eager to see him, to hear from his lips the strange happenings of his life, the description of the foreign countries he had visited, tales about the great men he knew.

"When my feet first touched the earth which had mothered me," says he in describing the moment of his arrival,[29] "such a tremor ran through all my limbs, and such an emotion overpowered me, that I remained motionless for some time, and I do not know how long I would have continued thus, if I had not heard from a window a voice which sweetly swept through my heart and which I seemed to recognize. I had alighted from the stage-coach a short distance from the house so that

[27] *Memorie*, vol. i, p. 241.
[28] *Cours fam. de Lit.*, tome v, p. 420. And in another passage (pp. 407-8) he adds: "Dans les Confidences de Saint Augustin, si tendre et si pieux pour sa mère, il n'y a pas beaucoup de pages en littérature intime supérieures a ce retour d'un fils aventurier dans la maison paternelle."
[29] *Memorie*, vol. i, p. 209.

the noise of the wheels might not give warning of my approach. When, after having knocked at the door, I heard somebody asking from above: 'Who is there?' I tried to disguise my voice and answered only: 'Open.' That one word was enough to reveal my identity to one of my sisters and, turning to the others, she shouted: 'It is Lorenzo!' They all came dashing down the stairs, threw themselves into my arms, almost suffocated me with caresses and kisses, and led me to my father, whose emotion I can hardly describe."

That night and the following day he spent at home, while the house was crowded with admiring friends and acquaintances, who fêted him as the most famous son of the town. On November 4th, however, he had to leave reluctantly to meet Nancy in Treviso and, planning to return with her in a few days, he took with him his brother Paolo and the youngest of his sisters, Faustina. In that city, however, he changed his mind, and after nearly a week spent in renewing all his old friendships[30] he sent his wife to Ceneda in company with the other two and went to Venice, ostensibly for the purpose of engaging the singers for the Drury Lane Theatre but in reality because he longed to find himself once again in the atmosphere of his adventurous youth.

But Venice had undergone a sad change. Delivered to the Austrians by Napoleon, it had lost all its past splendor and frivolous gayety, and when Lorenzo reached there he found the streets deserted, the cafés abandoned, all the theatres closed: it seemed as though the population were panic-stricken. Alas! The martyrdom of the betrayed city had only begun.

[30] There he met also Bernardo Memmo. "Teresa," he says, "was still with him. A widow, homely, fat and aged, she was still that man's idol and the absolute mistress of his will!"

There Da Ponte's only occupation appears to have been that of trying to gather up the threads of his old romances. He found out that Angela Tiepolo had died; saw her brother, who through his dissipation had been reduced to the condition of a beggar; met again the prima donna "Ferrarese" on whose account he had lost his position in Vienna; and even tried to renew his old love affair with that Angioletta Bellaudi whose family had provoked his banishment in 1779.

This cost him dear, for the same Gabriello Doria, Angioletta's brother-in-law, who in the past had been his accuser, denounced him to the Austrian police and one night he received the peremptory order to leave the city and Venetian territory within twenty-four hours.[31]

Being thus prevented from returning to his home town—which he was to see no more—he sent a messenger to Ceneda to inform his wife that she should hurriedly meet him in Padua. From that city, after encountering further difficulties with the Austrian authorities, by whom Nancy was even suspected of being a French spy, they proceeded by way of Ferrara to Bologna. There, we are told, Da Ponte had the good fortune to meet Ugo Foscolo,—which is not at all unlikely since the great poet was actually there at that time.[32]

Meanwhile, being reminded of the purpose of his

---

[31] In the *Memorie* it is stated (vol. i, p. 228) that he was ordered to leave the city. Probably, however, that order included also the Venetian State, otherwise why should he not have returned to Ceneda?

[32] He was writing in September and October 1798 some articles (*Istruzioni politico-morali*) for the *Genio democratico* and the *Monitore bolognese* of that city. Nicolini, Notes to the *Memorie*, vol. ii, p. 303.

journey by a letter from Taylor, Lorenzo started to search for suitable artists. Being unsuccessful in locating any in that city, he decided to leave his wife there in order that she might not be exposed to the hardships of another journey, and left for Florence.

There again he had no luck as far as his mission was concerned, if indeed he gave any of his attention to it, and, after several days spent in amusements, he returned to Bologna, where finally, through the assistance of an agent, he was able to engage the soprano Allegranti[33] and the tenor Damiani.[34]

With them and their families, Nancy and the young son of Signora Banti, our Poet started at once on his way back to England. The party, however, were detained in Hamburg for over a month owing to the fact that the harbor was ice-bound, and only in the first days of March landed in Dover.

Lorenzo's meeting with Taylor was anything but pleasant. He was severely criticized for his long delay in returning and, as for the singers he had engaged, Signora Allegranti was found to be too old, and Damiani only a second-rate tenor.

The events which followed are related in the *Memorie* in a most confused manner. Probably the story should run thus:[35] Having some money on his arrival in London, Da Ponte set up a little printing shop

---

[33] Maddalena Allegranti (?-?) could not have been in her prime when Da Ponte engaged her, in 1799, for she sang for the first time in Venice in 1771. She had already been in England in 1781. Her voice, though thin, was extremely sweet.

[34] Natale Damiani never was a great singer. He appeared in secondary parts at San Carlo, in Naples, and at San Benedetto, in Venice.

[35] Nicolini's version (Notes to the *Memorie*, vol. ii, pp. 304-5) is here followed closely as the only one which offers a clear solution of our Poet's hazy and often contradictory statements.

which seemed to be in the way of becoming a successful enterprise.[36] Taylor's curiosity being aroused, he requested that he might be allowed to see the place, a request which for some reason Lorenzo saw fit to deny. This and the Poet's evident prosperity gave rise to suspicions on the impresario's part and, through a lawyer, he demanded an accounting of all the money which Lorenzo had handled for him from the beginning of their business relations. After long litigation, it was found—at least according to what is stated in the *Memorie*—that there was a balance in favor of Da Ponte of two hundred and fifty guineas. Either because he believed that more was due to him, or because he had taken offense at the legal proceedings, our Poet resorted then to one of his customary retaliations by printing a libel against Taylor,[37] the publication of which the latter prevented only by paying, through a third party, a bribe of fifty guineas. As a natural consequence Da Ponte was dismissed from his position at the Drury Lane Theatre.

This must have occurred towards the beginning of 1800. That he was entirely without funds, as he states,[38] seems hardly probable, since about that time (February 18th) he wrote to his brother Paolo to join him in London (which the young man did) offering him a position in a piano factory in which he had an interest.[39]

His next move was to open an Italian book-store

---

[36] Among other publications, he turned out, for Leonardo Nardini, an expurgated edition of *Orlando Furioso*. *Memorie*, vol. i, p. 265.
[37] *Memorie*, vol. i, p. 245.
[38] *Ibid.*, vol. i, p. 247.
[39] The letter was published by Domenico Giurati, in his article *Su Lorenzo Da Ponte a proposito del Don Giovanni* in the *Illustrazione Italiana*, vol xxiv, No. 2, Jan. 10th, 1897. See also Nicolini, Notes to the *Memorie*, vol. ii, p. 305.

in Haymarket which also seems to have prospered since he informs us that by March 1st, 1801, his stock had increased to nine hundred volumes. It was in connection with this business venture that he had an opportunity of becoming acquainted with the English poet and scholar, Thomas Mathias,[40] who throughout his life remained his constant friend.

But this apparent prosperity was short-lived, for on March 10th of that same year—he reminds us that it was his fifty-second birthday[41]—he was arrested for a note which he had endorsed for Taylor, who not only had failed to honor it, but was now able by virtue of his position as an M. P. to escape apprehension. No sooner had he been bailed out on the following morning than two more summonses of the same nature were served on him, so that in twenty-four hours he was arrested three times. "But this," says he facetiously,[42] "was only the prelude to the *strepitosissima* symphony played on me for more than three months by Banti, Federici, Taylor, the usurers, the lawyers

---

[40] Thomas James Mathias (1754?-1835) belonged to a distinguished English family. After studying at Eton, he entered Cambridge in 1770, where he became a close friend of Spencer and Perceval. In 1782 he was appointed sub-treasurer to the Queen and in 1812 librarian at Buckingham Palace. Five years later, however, on account of his ill health, he settled in Naples, where he spent the remainder of his life "in love with the climate and the language," and where he entertained his friend Sir Walter Scott when the latter, during his last illness, came to Italy. Mathias' most important literary production is his *Pursuits of Literature* (1794-98), a reckless satire against men of letters. He wrote also a number of odes, epistles in verse, and other satires besides the one mentioned. But his greatest achievement was that of being perhaps the best English scholar in Italian since the time of Milton. In Italian he wrote *Poesie Liriche* and *Canzoni Toscane*, besides editing with scholarly prefaces and notes many Italian classics.

[41] *Memorie*, vol. i, p. 243.
[42] *Ibid.*

DA PONTE'S LONDON CAREER

and the officers of all the courts of London, by whom I was arrested no less than thirty times during that period on account of Taylor's debts." The consequence was that he had to declare himself bankrupt.

How, after this, he was able to reopen his bookstore, remains a mystery,—unless we assume that as early as 1801, or at the latest towards the beginning of 1802, he had entered into that disastrous partnership with a certain Nardini to which he refers a few pages further on in his autobiography.[43] The fact is, according to his statement, that he was publishing in 1802 a reprint of his *Saggi poetici* and an expurgated edition of Casti's *Animali parlanti,* while at the same time enjoying a fair amount of prosperity through his book-selling.[44]

It was in that same year that he had the pleasure of seeing again his boyhood friend, Colombo, who came to London accompanying as a tutor two young Italian noblemen on an educational trip.

But the most momentous event for him, in this period, was his reinstatement as poet to the Drury Lane Theatre, an unexpected good fortune which he attributes in his *Memorie*[45] to the fact that the creditors of the theatre, "dissatisfied with Taylor's management," had entrusted it to other hands, while

---

[43] *Memorie*, vol. i, p. 261.
[44] Did he really publish the edition of Casti's poem to which he alludes? Nicolini (Notes to the *Memorie*, vol. ii, p. 307) very strongly doubts it, asserting that the only known edition of the *Animali parlanti* bearing a London imprint is that of 1822, which, however, was clandestinely printed in Florence. He is of the opinion that the curious letter by Casti published in Lorenzo's autobiography, in which a strong protest is made against the expurgation and annotation of the poem, justifies the suspicion that the whole thing was only a "bluff" staged by Da Ponte for the purpose of tormenting his old "rival."
[45] Vol. i, pp. 253-4.

the impresario, following Banti's retirement from the stage, had gone to Paris, remaining there for some time, "for reasons," he adds, "which it is not necessary to state." These reasons so mysteriously alluded to, are, however, revealed by the Poet a few pages later on, where it is disclosed that Taylor, having ceased being an M. P., was liable to arrest for debt.[46]

But is the assertion that the management of the Drury Lane Theatre had changed hands, correct? Hardly; for we soon find Lorenzo entangled again in litigation with the same Taylor, who appears to be still the impresario. It is more likely, therefore, that the change of administration was only apparent and that Gould (the man who recalled Da Ponte to his former position) was acting only temporarily as manager, during the absence of Taylor. At any rate, Lorenzo resumed his poetical tasks and in 1803 wrote the libretto of *Castore e Polluce o Il trionfo dell' amor fraterno,* the music of which was composed by Winter.[47] It was a decided success, which the following year was at least equalled when the other opera was given, *Il ratto di Proserpina,* the fruit also of Da Ponte's collaboration with the German composer.

Meanwhile, however, Lorenzo's financial circumstances were going from bad to worse. Unpaid notes he had endorsed for Taylor and other people had to be

---

[46] *Memorie,* vol. i, p. 256.

[47] Peter Winter (1755-1825), born at Mannheim, after playing in the Kapelle of the Elector of Bavaria, became in 1776 director of the Munich Court Theatre, where he started his career as an operatic composer. His most popular work, *Das unterbrochene Opferfest,* was produced in Vienna in 1796. In 1803 he left Germany for England. In London his works gained for him an undeniable prestige, *Castore e Polluce, Il ratto di Proserpina* and *Zaira* being considered his masterpieces. He composed altogether about 30 operas.

met almost daily, and, as if this had not been sufficient to worry him, he plunged into a more hazardous speculation, taking over the share of his partner Nardini, and thus augmenting the number of his creditors. Legal proceedings—the man must have been a familiar figure in London courts—and lawyers' fees consumed his scant resources, while ultimate disaster was only delayed, not averted.

Foreseeing what the outcome would be, he then decided to send his wife and children to America (where Nancy's people had settled) ostensibly for a visit, but with the evident purpose of joining her later on and starting life anew under more favorable auspices. It is peculiarly significant that Nancy carried with her the not inconsiderable sum of six or seven thousand dollars, which he claims was the fruit of her own savings[48] but which at any rate was rescued from any possible claim on the part of his creditors.

When the day set for their departure arrived—September 20th, 1804—Da Ponte went to see them off at Gravesend. How the Poet felt when he saw his dear ones on that boat which was to carry them beyond the ocean, is best told by him.

"In the moment," he says,[49] "in which I gave my wife my last embrace and farewell, and when I glanced for the last time at her and those four children of ours, it seemed to me as though an icy hand tore my heart from my breast. My grief was such that for more than half an hour I remained in doubt whether I should bring my family back to London or sail for America myself, trusting the rest to Providence."

Here a question arises: how many children altogether had Lorenzo, and who were the four who sailed

[48] *Memorie*, vol. ii, p. 6.   [49] *Ibid.*, vol. i, p. 270.

from England with their mother? Very little could be said on this point, were the *Memorie* the only source of information. Fortunately some of Da Ponte's letters partly solve the problem.

In one that he wrote to Michele Colombo on August 1st, 1828,[50] he says:

"I could tell you a great deal about my family, and more sad news than good tidings. Of the two little girls you saw, the older died at the age of 28, leaving a daughter who is her perfect image, in beauty, grace and talents.—The second, whom you know, is also very beautiful, so they say, and very gifted, but she has had no luck. She had for more than three years a parasite of a husband, and on account of his vices was obliged to ask for a divorce. She obtained it, and for the last seven years has been living with me.—The lively boy whom you saw, died before reaching his twenty-first year."

Of the two daughters nothing else is known, except that the name of the first one seems to have been Luigia.[51] The boy referred to is Giuseppe, about whom there will be occasion to speak later. These three children Colombo saw during his visit to London in 1802; the fourth child who sailed with Nancy —about whom the Poet says that he was only one year old[52]—was undoubtedly the second son, named Lorenzo, after his father; for other records confirm that he was born in London.[53]

---

[50] Bernardi, *L. Da Ponte*, p. 183.

[51] The name appears in one of the letters written to Lorenzo by his New York pupils and appended to the last volume of the *Memorie*, as specimens of their efficiency in Italian. It bears the date of April 20th, 1829, and is signed F. S.

[52] *Memorie*, vol. i, p. 270.

[53] Lorenzo L. Da Ponte, the Poet's second son, was for several years a professor of Italian literature in the University of the City of New York, now New York University. Besides editing, in collaboration with others, a few works of general erudition, he published in 1833 *A History of the Flor-*

As for the children born in America, none is mentioned by name in the *Memorie,* though there are allusions to a third boy, Carlo.[54] Of him, however, as well as of two daughters, Matilde and Fanny, mention is often found in Da Ponte's letters.

After his family's departure, Lorenzo remained in London only six months longer, during which he tried in vain to straighten out his business affairs. They were, however, through the many responsibilities he had incurred, in so tangled a condition that, after a few months of struggle, he was obliged to assemble all his creditors, in the hope of reaching some sort of a settlement. The meeting, according to the *Memorie,*[55] took place on the evening of March 1st, 1805, but ended without any agreement being arrived at.

Having been informed, late the following night, by a friendly officer of the court, that it was planned to have him arrested the next morning, Da Ponte made his escape. Before dawn he left his home, and within a few hours after collecting from the management of the Drury Lane Theatre a sum due to him, he was able to secure passage on a boat scheduled to sail for Philadelphia on the 5th of the month.

---

entine Republic and of the Age and Rule of the Medici, which is often erroneously attributed to his father. From what has been stated above, there seems to be no doubt that Prof. Da Ponte was born in 1803, and the "notices, official and otherwise" alluded to by Krehbiel (*Music and Manners,* p. 171) which point to 1805 as the year of his birth, must be incorrect. Prof. L. L. Da Ponte married Miss Cornelia Durant of Philadelphia, a niece of President Monroe, became the father of one child, Durant, and died in 1840. Durant Da Ponte, who died in 1894, was married twice. Two sons, Lorenzo and Enrico Da Ponte, were born of the first marriage; of the second, only a son, Serill (Marchesan, *L. Da Ponte,* p. 482).

[54] Vol. ii, pp. 50 and 61.
[55] Vol. i, p. 274.

Where he spent those few days, we are not told; probably hidden somewhere in London. The fact is that, without any unpleasant incident, he got away from England, saddened only by his pathetic leavetaking from his brother Paolo, who accompanied him to Gravesend. The boy, whose only consolation was Lorenzo's promise that he should shortly join him in America, died in London two years later.

CHAPTER VI

IN AMERICA

Lorenzo's journey to America was not exactly what one would call pleasant. Even the scant comforts afforded by the sailing vessels of that period were not his lot, for it was probably a freight-boat on which he took passage, since he and one other man were the only passengers.[1] As for the sleeping accommodations he found there, it is enough to state that, having neglected to bring a mattress with him, he was obliged to make a substitute for a bed with his linen and clothes, in order not to lie on the hard wooden cot.

But what was most provoking to him, was evidently the scarcity and poor quality of the food. With that rather amusing resentment peculiar to him when he thought he had a grievance against anybody, he did not hesitate to affirm that Captain Hayden, the skipper of the boat—that *mariuolo* of Nantucket,—was the meanest man on earth.

After nearly three months[2] of this undelightful voyage, he finally landed in Philadelphia on the morning of June 4th, 1805. Having learned in that city that his family had moved to New York, he hastened there and early the next morning was already with his wife and children. His idea now was to start in

---

[1] For details of this journey, see *Memorie*, vol. ii, pp. 3-5.
[2] Da Ponte states (*Memorie*, vol. ii, p. 3) that his trip lasted 86 days. If this be true, he sailed on March 10th, not on March 5th, otherwise his voyage lasted 91, not 86 days.

business with part of the money Nancy had brought with her. Following her father's advice, he opened a little grocery.

"Let any one who has a sense of humor," says he in a whimsical mood at this point of his *Memorie*,[3] "imagine how I laughed at myself whenever my poetical hand was obliged to weigh two ounces of tea or to measure half a yard of 'pigtail' for a cobbler or a teamster, or to pour for him a three cent 'morning dram,' which, of course, had nothing in common with my other dramas, *Una cosa rara* or *Le nozze di Figaro* for instance."

Undoubtedly it was a vastly different life from the one he had led at the court of Joseph II or in his London operatic career. Yet he was not unhappy, for his inborn cheerfulness never abandoned him and, as he informs us, the little business was thriving. But unfortunately this state of affairs did not last long. In September of that year an epidemic of yellow fever broke out in New York, which decided him to dispose of his grocery-store and move with his family to Elizabethtown, N. J.

There he bought a house, with a little land, while continuing the same traffic in which he had engaged in New York. But, alas! our Poet was not cut out to be a tradesman, and in little more than a year, disgusted with his venture, he had to give it up.

Only his own words can adequately convey an idea of his unique business methods:

"Sometimes deceived by feigned distress, sometimes by false promises, I sold my goods to those who were never prepared when their payments became due. I lent my money, my credit, my effects to persons who studied at night how they might overreach me in the day. I delivered from the hands of the sheriff or freed from prison those who rewarded me with insult and abuse; I parted

[3] Vol. ii, p. 6.

with my property to assist in the furnishing of stores, in the purchase of lands, in the building of houses for perfidious people who by covert practices were attempting my ruin. I was sometimes obliged, rather than lose all, to take, for notes due long before, lame horses, broken carts, disjointed chairs, old shoes, rancid butter, watery cider, rotten eggs, apples, brooms, turnips, potatoes."[4]

This highly colored narrative must not, of course, be taken literally; we are already acquainted with Lorenzo's foible for posing as a victim of human perfidy. As one of his biographers appropriately remarks, "in his books those who owed him money are all unconscionable scoundrels and cheats, and those to whom he owes money are all merciless, grasping skinflints who sold him bad goods."[5]

In order to pay his debts, he was obliged, after selling his store, to dispose also of the little house which he had thought would prove a peaceful retreat for his old age; and towards the beginning of 1807 he returned with his wife and children to New York.

One cannot help feeling a certain admiration for the indomitable courage of this man who, now nearly sixty years of age and with a large family to support, was about to start again in a new line of activity, that of teaching his native language in a city where, to use his own words, "it was no better known than Turkish or Chinese."[6]

The only encouragement he had received was a vague promise of assistance given him by a bookseller named Riley. Through him, however, he had the good fortune of becoming acquainted, soon after his return, with a young man of great talent, belonging to a fam-

---

[4] *Compendium of the Life of Lorenzo Da Ponte, written by himself.* New York, Riley, 1807.
[5] Krehbiel, *Music and Manners*, p. 172.
[6] *Memorie*, vol. ii, p. 9.

ily of distinguished scholars, Clement Clarke Moore,[7] who later became the recognized pioneer of Hebrew lexicography in the United States, and who endeared himself to children for all time as the author of " 'Twas the Night before Christmas."

Fascinated by the quaint personality of the old Poet, Moore decided to form a little class in Italian, and presently Da Ponte began teaching in the house of Bishop Moore,[8] his first four pupils. Their names he commemorates with deep attachment in his autobiography.[9] They were, besides his young friend, Clement C. Moore, the latter's cousin Nathaniel Moore,[10] John McVickar and E. Pendleton. From this

[7] Clement Clarke Moore (1779-1863), son of Bishop Benjamin Moore who was president of Columbia College from 1801 to 1811, was born and educated in New York City. He graduated from Columbia in 1798 and, although trained for the ministry, never took orders, but devoted himself mainly to oriental and classical literature. He was a professor of biblical learning and later of Oriental and Greek literatures in the General Theological Seminary. His name is associated with the following works: *Hebrew and Greek Lexicon*, the first of the kind in America; *Bishop B. Moore's Sermons; Poems; George Castriot, surnamed Scanderbeg, King of Albania*.

[8] Bishop Benjamin Moore (1748-1816) was born in Newtown, Long Island. After completing his studies in King's College (now Columbia University) he started to teach Greek and Latin, while preparing to enter the ministry. After spending a few years in England, he was ordained in London and, on his return to New York (1800), was made rector of Trinity parish. The following year, after the resignation of Bishop Provoost, he was unanimously elected to succeed him. Almost contemporaneously he was appointed President of Columbia College, in which capacity he remained up to 1811, when, attacked by paralysis, he retired from further active service.

[9] *Memorie*, vol. ii, p. 10.

[10] Nathaniel F. Moore (1782-1872) was a nephew of Bishop B. Moore. He graduated from Columbia in 1802, studied law, was admitted to the bar in 1805 and practiced for a few years. In 1817 he was appointed adjunct professor of Greek and Latin in his Alma Mater, and three years later promoted to a full professorship. From 1835 to 1837 he was in Europe,

small beginning, through the help of his influential patrons, he was able in a short time to enroll large classes of young men and young women, all eager to acquire from him the command of his native tongue. This was something novel in New York, but later it became a fashionable accomplishment. Da Ponte, as though his youth were renewed, threw himself heart and soul into his Italian teaching, ordering books from Italy, arranging little plays to be performed by his pupils in his home, and holding weekly receptions at which Italian classics were read and discussed. On the occasion of the first of these receptions he distributed to his guests the already quoted pamphlet, *Compendium of the Life of Lorenzo Da Ponte, written by himself.*

But though so unexpectedly successful, and in spite of his former disastrous experiences, our Poet had not entirely given up his hope of attaining an independent position through some kind of commercial enterprise. As soon as he had accumulated a little money, he entered into a partnership with a distiller who had led him to believe that a fortune could soon be amassed in the enterprise. As might be expected, in this case also he met with "deceit and treachery" and, to quote his own words he "even felt tempted to leave New York, to avoid seeing that *malandrino.*"[11]

While he was in this unpleasant frame of mind, which was not assuaged by the fact that the number of his pupils had momentarily diminished, he received

---

on his return assumed the duties of librarian in Columbia, continuing in this position till 1842 when he became President of the college, an office which he held up to 1849. His most important publications are: *Remarks on the Pronunciation of the Greek Language; Ancient Mineralogy; Lectures on the Greek Language and Literature;* and *Historical Sketch of Columbia College.*

[11] *Memorie*, vol. ii, p. 14.

a letter from Nancy's relatives containing a glowing description of the natural beauties and exceptional business opportunities of the town of Sunbury, Pa., where they had settled. With his usual impulsiveness, he decided then to go there with his family, his mind being already made up that there perhaps he could find peace and prosperity.

They left New York on June 10th, 1811,[12] and on their arrival in Sunbury were received as guests by Nancy's sister. Lorenzo's impressions after a few days spent in the pretty little town were so favorable that he determined to establish his home there. "I had saved from three to four thousand dollars," he says (which proves, by the way, that his venture as a distiller had not been entirely without profit), "and I thought that with one ounce of good luck and two of common sense I might be able, through some kind of business, to earn enough to keep my family in comfort."[13]

So he returned alone to New York, settled up his affairs, and went back to Sunbury, where he engaged at once in several lines of trade. From his *Memorie*—the only source of information concerning this period of his life—it appears that, besides dealing in groceries, he handled also widely different lines, such as wheat, distilled liquors and medical supplies,—the latter on the advice of his brother-in-law, who was a physician.

During the first years, everything prospered and he even found time to give Italian lessons to young ladies in Sunbury and the near-by town of Northumberland. He gained the esteem and friendship of the principal families of the place, among whom he gratefully recalls the Grants, Halls, Bujers and Smiths.

[12] *Memorie*, vol. ii, p. 14.   [13] *Ibid.*

But this peaceful interlude was not of long duration, for with his customary lack of caution he began once more to sell on credit, thus becoming entangled in innumerable financial difficulties and endless litigation. For all this he blames principally, in his autobiography,[14] his brother-in-law, Dr. Grahl, on whose advice alone he says he trusted worthless persons, and whom he even accuses of having materially benefited by his troubles.

Still another instance in which Lorenzo betrays ill-feeling against his wife's relatives, is when he informs the reader of the death of Nancy's sister, which occurred during the latter part of his stay in Sunbury, when his affairs were in a desperate condition. Not satisfied with accusing the dead woman of having entertained "an unjust hate" towards him, and of having taken "an ill-advised revenge" by ignoring his family in her will (she died a widow without children), he goes so far as to assert that a good part of her $15,000 estate was in reality money entrusted to her keeping by Nancy, who thus was defrauded by one of her own flesh and blood in a moment of greatest need.[15]

How little of truth there is in these accusations, can easily be ascertained from the contents of a letter which the present writer was fortunate enough to discover in the Manuscript Department of the New York Public Library[16] and which is reproduced in Appendix I of this volume (at p. 141). The letter, written by Da Ponte on November 7th, 1824, to an unknown person in Sunbury, discloses that not only did Nancy receive from her sister a legacy the interest of which was suf-

[14] *Memorie*, vol. ii, p. 21.
[15] *Ibid.*, vol. ii, p. 31.
[16] Addis Emmet Collection.

ficient to pay the family rent, but that some of his children also were remembered in their aunt's will.

To dwell on all the details of Lorenzo's misfortunes and disappointments in Sunbury, would hardly be worth while, especially since only his side could be presented. In his *Memorie* it is the same old story of rapacious creditors and rascally debtors, all in a conspiracy to ruin him, while even in his own household he is unscrupulously robbed by people in his employ.

As one of his biographers puts it, "there is something so exaggerated in the style of the complaint, and so petty in the nature of the grievances, that the 'pity of it' is almost lost in a kind of serio-comedy."[17] It may suffice to state that things went from bad to worse, reaching a climax in 1818, when, having lost all he had, he saw even his household furniture seized by the sheriff.

In the autumn of that year he went alone to Philadelphia, with the intention of devoting himself to the diffusion of a knowledge of the Italian language and literature. To attain his end he acquired, partly on credit, partly by engaging his last resources, a considerable number of Italian volumes, hoping that a vague promise given him by the public librarian of that city would be fulfilled and his collection of books purchased for the library.

Unfortunately for our Poet, a lack of library funds prevented this, and he saw nothing left for him to do but to return to his family in Sunbury and send his oldest son Giuseppe with the books to New York, on the chance of being able to dispose of them among his old pupils. This the boy successfully accomplished and, on his return, brought back to his father, together

---

[17] Tuckerman, *L. Da Ponte*.

with the money he had obtained, a letter from Clement
C. Moore urging him to establish himself once more
in New York and resume his Italian classes. Accepting with enthusiasm this advice, which he calls
un' ispirazione celeste, he bade Sunbury *l'estremo addio*
and taking Giuseppe with him started on his way to
the Metropolis.

As Petrarch the day in which he first saw Laura, so
Da Ponte blessed the day, April 26th, 1819, when from
the Jersey shore he saw once again the island of Man-
hattan. Indeed it seems as though now for the first
time since his arrival in America he entered upon a
period of relative contentment. With a zeal which is
amazing when one considers that he had reached his
seventieth year, he at once resumed his lessons, reviv-
ing that ardent interest for the study of Italian which,
with unconcealed and pardonable pride, he repeatedly
asserts was awakened and stimulated by him alone.

Meeting with even a greater degree of success than
he had done years before, prior to his Sunbury venture, he was soon in a condition to recall his family
to New York and provide for the education of his
children. Giuseppe started studying law in Columbia
College, while the other two sons, Lorenzo and Carlo,[18]
were entrusted to a competent tutor. His classes were
frequented by many young men and some of the young
women of the most distinguished families of the city
and suburbs. His romantic past,—that is to say, *bien
entendu,* what was known of it—his genial personality
and his ardor, contributed a peculiar attraction to his
teaching.

---

[18] Little is known of this youngest son of Da Ponte. He
studied medicine (*Memorie*, vol. ii, p. 61) but it is doubtful
whether he ever practiced. We find him later associated
with his father in a book-store.

Gratefully he recalls in his *Memorie* all the kindness shown him by his pupils; of some of them he draws the most flattering pictures, of many he records the names; and a number of their letters to him, written in Italian, which are found appended to his autobiography, attest not only their unusual proficiency in that language, but also their warm attachment to their old professor.[19] Seldom indeed since that time have the Italian classics had so able and enthusiastic an exponent in the United States.

In the spring of 1821 Da Ponte lectured on Italy, defending the Italian national character from adverse criticism which had appeared in the English and American press at that time. Referring to this lecture, which was published later in pamphlet form, Dr. John W. Francis, a prominent New York physician and a personal friend of our Poet, makes the following comment:[20]

"A fair estimate may be formed of the great extent and variety of Da Ponte's knowledge, of his deep devotion to the mental capacity of Italy, his adoration of her language, and his laudations of her mighty authors, the strength, the copiousness and the sweetness of her language, and the fertility and special excellence of her divine music, by a perusal of his elaborate pamphlet, which he published in New York in 1821, entitled: *Sull' Italia, Discorso apologetico in risposta alla lettera dell' avvocato*

---

[19] A particularly brilliant and devoted student was Miss Fanny Leight, who later became Mrs. Cottenet and whom the Poet calls "the brightest gem of my Tuscan crown." Another pupil of his was Miss Virginia Brander, afterwards Mrs. Matthews, mother of Prof. Brander Matthews, from whom the writer received this information. And it might be of interest to the reader to learn that the poet Fitz-Greene Halleck also studied Italian under Da Ponte. (James Grant Wilson, *The Life and Letters of Fitz-Greene Halleck*, New York, Appleton, 1869, p. 282).

[20] *Old New York or Reminiscences of the past sixty years*, by John W. Francis (New York, Widdleton, 1866), p. 255.

LORENZO DA PONTE
FROM AN OLD PRINT.

Carlo Phillips. I was of the audience when Da Ponte delivered this discourse in English before a large assemblage, with the earnestness and animation of a great speaker. The work itself took its origin from the aspersions cast upon the Italian character by the English press, at the time when the English papers were filled with the details of the alleged corrupt conduct of Caroline, the queen consort of George the Fourth, and of the Italian witnesses. The copious stores of Da Ponte's reading can be estimated by a perusal of this vindication of his country and his countrymen. In reference to his native tongue he thus speaks: 'With her good fortune, Italy for five hundred years has preserved her charming language. That language which, for its united sweetness, delicacy, force and richness, compares with every ancient language, and surpasses every modern tongue; which equals in sublimity the Greek, the Latin in magnificence, in grandeur and conciseness the Hebrew, the German in boldness, in majesty the Spanish, and the English in energy. The language, in fine, which Providence bestowed on the Italians, because so perfectly adapted in its almost supernatural harmoniousness to the delicacy of their organs and perceptions, to the vivacity of their minds, and to the complexion of their ideas and sentiments, and which was formed so justly to illustrate their character.' This pamphlet by Da Ponte is well worth an attentive perusal at the present day, and is not to be classed among ephemeral productions."

One of the many good results which Lorenzo obtained from that lecture, was that of gaining the friendship of a young man, Henry James Anderson, who was pursuing his studies in New York, and who not only asked to be instructed in Italian, but begged the Poet to afford him lodging, as his family was living outside of the city. Shortly afterward, Anderson's two brothers and three other young men followed this example, and Da Ponte had the satisfaction of having, not without profit, this little group of resident students around him.

Some of these youths remained in his house for several years; one of them was Henry James Anderson himself, who in 1825 became professor of mathematics and astronomy in Columbia College, and who later married Da Ponte's youngest daughter, Fanny.[21] But just when all seemed turning out so well for him, the old Poet was plunged into the greatest depth of grief by the sudden death of his son Giuseppe, in his 21st year.

"I shall not relate," he says,[22] "the causes and the beginning of such a heart-breaking event, in order not to renew my anguish." And indeed it seems as though he never felt, not even when he later lost his wife, such an overwhelming sorrow. He was compelled to suspend his classes and, together with his family, left the city to be the guest of John R. Livingston[23]— whose three daughters he was instructing in Italian— at his summer home on the Hudson. There he em-

[21] This marriage very probably occurred some time after 1830, date of the second edition of the *Memorie*, for, had it taken place previously, Da Ponte would certainly not have failed to mention it. Prof. Anderson's connection with Columbia lasted up to 1843. He embraced the Catholic faith and died in 1875 at Lahore, India, where he had gone on a scientific commission. Fanny died in Paris, on Jan. 1st, 1844, while returning with her husband from Italy. She is buried in Père-La-Chaise. Dr. Anderson was but once married and left only two children, Elbert Ellery and Edward Henry, both now deceased. His living grandchildren are: P. Chauncey, Henry James, Harriet, J. Angela and Ellery O. Anderson, who is a prominent New York lawyer, to whose courtesy the writer is indebted for the above information.

[22] *Memorie*, vol. ii, p. 59.

[23] General James Grant Wilson, in his notes to *The Poetical Writings of Fitz-Greene Halleck*, (New York, Appleton, 1869), p. 383, refers to J. R. Livingston as "a wealthy gentleman who dispensed liberal hospitalities both at his city residence and at his country-seat on the Hudson." And adds: "Among the notabilities whom he entertained at the latter place was the Prince of Saxe-Weimar, who visited the United States in 1825-26."

ployed his leisure hours translating into Italian Byron's *Prophecy of Dante,* to which his attention had been called by some of his pupils.

"The sweet melancholy," he remarks,[24] "which pervades that poem from its very first page, did not console me in my distress but seemed rather to kindle and augment it. This, however, had in itself something so tender and pleasing that—I did not read—I devoured the first four cantos, without putting the book down. A certain analogy which, allowing for due proportion, I seemed to find between Dante's vicissitudes and my own, gave me the desire to translate that work into Italian verse."

Describing how he spent his days in that peaceful retreat, he adds:

"I used to get up at sunrise, would spend one hour reading either with my pupils or with my children an Italian author or poet, have breakfast with them, and then, resting under a peach or an apple tree, translate a passage of Byron's *Prophecy of Dante,* which caused me to weep sweet tears. When the inspiration seemed lacking, I hastened to renew it in the house of those three incomparable young ladies, who, with their pleasant reception, their divine enthusiasm for our authors, and their angellike faces, made me forget my anguish and spend happy moments in the pleasure of being their guest and teacher."[25]

Reinvigorated by this sojourn in the country, Lorenzo on his return to New York, besides resuming his classes, started to compile his autobiography, and planning to open an Italian bookstore ordered a considerable number of volumes from Europe.

In 1823 the first edition of his *Memorie* was published, and in the same year also came out a *Catalogo ragionato de' libri che si trovano al negozio di Lorenzo e Carlo Da Ponte,* from which it appears that his

[24] *Memorie,* vol. ii, p. 60.   [25] *Ibid.*

youngest son was his partner in the recently opened store.

Ever sensitive to any misconception in regard to Italy and her literature, he was incensed at a criticism of the Italian chivalric poetry—a youthful essay by the historian Prescott—which had been published in the *North American Review*.[26] His answer, in the form of a pamphlet,[27] brought out a second article by his opponent,[28] and the controversy, more amusing than conclusive, ended there.

While this was going on, Da Ponte, probably through the recommendation of his old pupil, Clement C. Moore, who at the time was a trustee of Columbia College, was appointed a professor of Italian literature in that instituton, then situated at the foot of Park Place, near Broadway. No salary was attached to the position. On the same basis adopted for other modern languages, which shortly before had been introduced in the college curriculum, Italian was admitted as an optional subject, and Lorenzo was to receive the fees of students who elected his courses.

[26] Prescott's article, which appeared in the October number of 1824 (vol. xix, p. 337), is a rather lengthy review of an English translation of Berni's *Orlando innamorato* and Ariosto's *Orlando furioso* by W. A. Rosa. A specimen of the type of criticism which aroused Lorenzo's indignation is the following: "It hardly seems possible that an enlightened people should long continue to take satisfaction in poems, founded on the same extravagant fictions, and spun out to the appalling length of twenty, thirty, nay forty cantos of a thousand verses each." In the same article Prescott gives expression to the following estimate of Thomas J. Mathias as a poet: "His poetical productions," he says, "rank with those of Milton in merit, and far exceed them in quality."

[27] *Alcune osservazioni sull' articolo quarto pubblicato nel "North American Review" il mese d' ottobre dell' anno 1824;* New York, Gray & Bunce, 1825.

[28] *The North American Review*, vol. xx, July, 1825.

COLUMBIA COLLEGE AT THE TIME OF DA PONTE'S PROFESSORSHIP
PARK PLACE, NEAR BROADWAY, NEW YORK.
"Drawn and Engraved expressly for the *New York Mirror*."

IN AMERICA

The following extracts from the minutes of the Trustees of Columbia College disclose the story of his connection with it:

May 2d, 1825. A letter from Mr. Da Ponte was received, asking permission to instruct the alumni of the College in the Italian language and to make use of some part of the building for that purpose. The above letter was referred to the Standing Committee.

June 6th, 1825. (At this meeting the report of the Standing Committee was laid on the table for further consideration.)

September 5th, 1825. *Resolved*, That a Professorship of Italian Literature be established in this College, but that the Professor be not considered one of the Board of the College, nor subject to the provisions of the second chapter of the statutes.

Resolved, That the attendance of the students upon said Professor be voluntary, and that the hours of attendance be appointed by the Professor, under the direction of the President.

Resolved, That Signore Da Ponte be and is hereby appointed to the said professorship, and that he be allowed to receive from the students who shall attend his lectures a reasonable compensation; but that no salary be allowed him from the College.

December 5th, 1825. (Da Ponte offers to sell two hundred and sixty-three volumes of Italian works to the college for $364.05. Referred to a committee, C. C. Moore, chairman.)

January 2d, 1826. (Favorable report; the books are bought for the library.)

January 5th, 1829. Ordered that $50 be paid to Signore Da Ponte in addition to what he has already been paid for making the catalogue of the College.

November 3d, 1829. (Da Ponte offers more books.)

November 12th, 1829. (Thirty-three volumes bought of Da Ponte for $140.)

November 30th, 1829. A proposition was received through the President from Signore Da Ponte, offering to add a number of Italian books to the College Library upon condition of his having a certain number of pupils provided him to instruct in the Italian language. Whereupon—

Resolved, That it is inexpedient to accept the proposition of Signore Da Ponte.[29]

What this proposition was, is explained in the last part of the *Memorie,* published in 1830.[30] To his great disappointment, Lorenzo had not been able to enroll even a single student in his Italian class. It seems that few of the young men selected the study of modern languages, and those who did showed a preference for French or Spanish. He proposed then that the College should require one hundred of them to register for an Italian course of eighty lessons, at a fee of $15, while he, on his part, obliged himself to present to the College one thousand volumes of selected Italian works, of a value equal to the total amount of the fees.

Of course, the offer, which would have involved a revision of the statutes, could not be entertained.

His friend Clement C. Moore, commenting on the unfeasibility of his proposal, in a letter reproduced by Da Ponte in his autobiography,[31] took him to task for what he interpreted as an overzealous desire to glorify himself. He wrote:

---

[29] These extracts were published for the first time by Krehbiel, in his essay on our Poet.
[30] Vol. ii, p. 134.
[31] *Ibid.* The letter, of course, is given by Da Ponte in Italian translation. Krehbiel, who reproduces a passage of it in his essay, translates Da Ponte's words back into English. The present author, however, has preferred to quote this same passage from the version given by Samuel Ward in his *Sketch*

"For what you have done for Italy and the cause of letters, so long as there remains a spark of taste among us for the belles-lettres, the name of Da Ponte, *clarum et venerabile nomen,* will be held in veneration; and his scholars of our, as well as of the gentler sex, will remember in the decline of life, the hours passed by them in pleasing conversation with their elegant and cultivated tutor, as among the sweetest moments of their existence; and it is therefore, my dear sir, that I pray you to let this suffice, and not aspire to acquire for yourself alone the whole glory of the universe."

There seems to be no doubt, judging from the way this failure is recorded in the *Memorie,* that Da Ponte took it, as well as Moore's rebuke, good-naturedly.

Already some years before he had jested about his empty title of professor, and in this connection it is perhaps worth while quoting here the following lines, with which he acknowledged an invitation to one of the annual banquets of the undergraduates:[32]

> Sum pastor sine ovibus,
> Arator sine bovibus,
> Hortulus sine flore,
> Lychnus sine splendore,
> Campus sine frumento,
> Crumena sine argento,
> Navita sine navibus,
> Ianua sine clavibus,
> Arbustus sine foliis,
> Taberna sine doliis,
> Olympus sine stellis,
> Chorea sine puellis,
> Artifex sine manibus,
> Venator sine canibus,

---

of the Life of L. D. P., published in the same year in which Lorenzo died (1838), for it is not unlikely that Ward had access to the original text.

[32] *Memorie*, vol. ii, pp. 88-89.

> Fons sine potatoribus,
> Pons sine viatoribus,
> Sacerdos sine templo,
> Professor sine exemplo.

As can be seen, despite his advanced age and all his misfortunes, his innate sense of humor had not deserted him.

CHAPTER VII

LAST YEARS

Towards the end of November 1825, the following announcement, which was to mark the beginning of a new era in the history of music in the United States, appeared in the New York papers:

"Signor Garcia respectfully announces to the American public that he has lately arrived in this country with an Italian *troupe* (among whom are some of the first artists of Europe), and has made arrangements with the Managers of the New-York Theatre to have the house on Tuesdays and Saturdays; on which nights the choicest Italian Operas will be performed, in a style which he flatters himself will give general satisfaction."

It was the introduction of Italian Opera in America.

The troupe, really a first-rate one, and perhaps the very best in those days, included, besides its leader Manuel Garcia,[1]—his wife, his son Manuel,[2] his

---

[1] Manuel Garcia (1775-1832) was a native of Seville. After studying under the best masters in that city, he sang for the first time in Cadiz, in an operetta which included songs of his own composition. His reputation as a singer was established after the success he attained soon after in Madrid. In 1808 he went to Paris and, after singing for a few seasons at the Théâtre des Italiens, moved to Italy, where he reached the highest degree of perfection in his art. In 1812 he sang in Naples in his opera *Il Califfo di Bagdad;* other operas he produced in various Italian cities, among which, perhaps the best, *La morte di Tasso* (1821) and *Il fazzoletto* (1823). From London, where he was from 1824, Garcia came to America in 1825, and in New York he gave his *La figlia dell' aria* (1827). He was also in Mexico and was about to return to Europe when robbed by brigands near Vera Cruz. His last years he spent in Paris, teaching. He wrote about 40 operas, none remarkable, and a *Metodo di canto*, still considered the best by competent vocalists.

[2] Manuel Garcia, Jr., (1805-1906), was born in Madrid.

daughter Maria[3] (afterwards famous under her married name of Malibran), Signora Barbieri, the baritone Angrisani, the basso Rossich, and Crivelli as a second tenor.

The season opened on the evening of November 29th with Rossini's *Barbiere,* attracting to the New York Theatre, better known as the Park Theatre,[4] an audience eager to enjoy what promised to be a new source of pleasure.

"An assemblage of ladies so fashionable, so numerous and so elegantly attired," the *Evening Post* of the following day records, "was probably never witnessed in our theatre;" and among those present were—according to James Grant Wilson,[5]—Joseph Bonaparte,

---

He was a professor at the Paris *Conservatoire* from 1830 to 1848, from which year to 1893 he held a similar position at the Royal Academy of Music in London. He acquired great fame both as an exponent of the *bel canto* and as the inventor of the laryngoscope (1850).

[3] Maria Felicia Garcia Malibran (1808-36), born in Paris when her father was singing there, was one of the most beautiful and most gifted singers who ever appeared on the stage. Her voice, full of charm and of a phenomenal range, enabled her to sing both the soprano and contralto parts. Under her father's expert guidance, she was able to appear, when only 17, at Covent Garden, taking the place of Signora Pasta, indisposed. She came to New York with the rest of the Garcia troupe, sang in *Otello, Barbiere, Don Giovanni, Romeo e Giulietta* and *Tancredi,* and there she married Malibran, a French banker much older than she. In 1828 she returned alone to Europe, and was received with unbounded enthusiasm in Paris and in several Italian cities. Having obtained a divorce, she married in 1835 a Belgian violinist, Charles de Bériot; but her happiness was short-lived, for she died the following year. She inspired some of the best stanzas of Alfred de Musset.

[4] It was located at Park Row, at what is now numbered 21 to 25. Opened in 1798, the theatre was burned in 1820; was rebuilt a year later, and finally destroyed, again by fire, in 1848. For fifty years it was one of the most prominent play-houses in New York.

[5] *Life and Letters of Fitz-Greene Halleck,* p. 282.

THEATRE.

ITALIAN OPERA.—SIGNOR GARCIA respectfully announces to the American public, that he has lately arrived in this country with an Italian *troupe*, (among whom are some of the first artists of Europe) and has made arrangements with the Managers of the NEW-YORK THEATRE, to have the house on Tuesdays and Saturdays; on which nights the choicest Italian Operas will be performed, in a style which he flatters himself will give general satisfaction.

THIS EVENING, Nov. 29, will be performed for the first time in America, the Italian opera of
"IL BARBIERA DI SEVIGLIA."

Rosina,	Signorina Garcia
Berta,	Signora Garcia
Count Almaviva,	Signor Garcia
Don Basilio,	Angrizani
Don Bartolo,	Rosich
Figaro,	Garcia jr.
Fiorello,	Crevelli

Box tickets will be two dollars, and Pit one dollar. On the opera nights a limited number of Gallery tickets will be issued for the accommodation of the frequenters of that part of the Theatre, at the original price of twenty-five cents.

Pit tickets for the opera may be obtained during days of performance at the Box office.

Tickets of the permanent boxes will be transferable.

Gentlemen having permanent boxes or seats for the season, are requested to call at the Box office on Monday or Tuesday, between 10 and 3 o'clock, to settle their subscriptions.

Certificates for seats during the season will be issued every morning of the opera from the Box office.

Books of the opera can be procured at the Theatre—price 37½ cents.

The doors will be opened at half past 7—and performance to commence at 8 o'clock precisely.

CHATHAM THEATRE.——OPERA NIGHT.
THIS EVENING, Nov. 29, the opera
THE DEVIL'S BRIDGE

THE BEGINNING OF ITALIAN OPERA IN AMERICA

FACSIMILE OF THE ANNOUNCEMENT OF THE FIRST PERFORMANCE OF "IL BARBIERE DI SIVIGLIA" IN NEW YORK.

From the *Evening Post* of November 29, 1825.

the ex-king of Spain, and the two friends, Fenimore Cooper and Fitz-Greene Halleck, who sat side by side.

The opera was accounted a triumph, as may be gathered from the quaint comments of the press:

"In what language," the above mentioned daily remarks, "shall we speak of an entertainment so novel in this country, but which has so long ranked as the most elegant and refined among the amusements of the higher classes of the old world? All have obtained a general idea of the opera from report. But report can give but a faint idea of it. Until it is seen, it will never be believed that a play can be conducted in recitative or singing and yet appear nearly as natural as the ordinary drama. We were last night surprised, delighted, enchanted, and such were the feelings of all who witnessed the performance. The repeated plaudits with which the theatre rang, were unequivocal, unaffected bursts of rapture."

The *Albion, or British Colonial and Foreign Weekly Gazette* published the following:

"We have been disappointed in not receiving a scientific critique which we were promised from a professor on the Italian opera of Tuesday night; we shall, however, have something to say later and meanwhile can state that the experiment has proved completely successful and the *troupe* may be assured of making a fortunate campaign."

It is easy to imagine with what feelings Da Ponte witnessed this triumph of Italian art. He was one of Garcia's earliest visitors. The story of their meeting runs thus: Lorenzo introduced himself as the author of *Don Giovanni* ("my *Don Giovanni*", as he was fond of saying) and Garcia, clasping him in his arms, danced about the room like a child, singing *Fin ch'han del vino*,—the famous drinking song of Mozart's masterpiece.[6]

[6] See Krehbiel, *Music and Manners*, p. 178.

At the Poet's suggestion, Garcia decided to include *Don Giovanni* in the season's repertoire. The only objection raised was the lack of a suitable artist for the part of Don Ottavio, but this the ever-resourceful Da Ponte overcame by pledging himself to furnish the required singer. This he did through the financial help of some of his friends and pupils. The opera was performed for the first time on the evening of May 23d, 1826, and after a clamorous success was repeated three more times in the course of that season.

How little prepared the press was to cope with operatic criticism, may be judged by the remarks one reads in the already quoted *Albion*. Its editor, who after the first performance of the season, as will be remembered, regretted his inability to discuss the qualites of Rossini's music, owing to the fact that he had failed to receive the "scientific critique which we were promised from a professor," now states that "to enter into any minute examination of *Don Giovanni's* scientific merits is beyond our space and purpose." We read later that "Madame Barbieri's taste is pure and her science considerable," and that "Garcia Senior is not at home in the simple melodies of Mozart." Why? Very simple! "He must have," this very scientific critic explains, "a wide field for display: he must have ample room to verge enough for unlimited curvetings and flourishes." Maria, on the other hand, was almost up to his requirements, for he writes: "Mlle Garcia's Zerlina, though not so simple and rustic as Fedors [*sic*], the great Zerlina of Europe, is much more pleasing and fascinating."[7]

While all this was going on, Lorenzo was still strug-

---

[7] Evidently he means Josephine Fodor-Mainvielle.

MADAME MALIBRAN GARCIA
FROM AN ENGRAVING BY C. G. CHILD.

gling with his classes, his book-store, his family troubles and the inevitable debts.

Yet he found time to write a few articles interpreting certain passages in the *Divine Comedy,* which appeared in a New York magazine in 1825,[8] and to publish, in 1827, a *Storia della lingua e letteratura italiana in New York,* which is a sort of panegyric of his own work as a teacher.

On February 18th, 1830,[9] came from Italy his half-brother Agostino together with his daughter, Giulia, a young singer who had successfully made her début in Venice some time before.

Our Poet had long cherished a desire to see his only surviving brother, Agostino. As early as 1825 —that is, at the time of Garcia's arrival in the United States—he had urged him and his daughter to come to America, hoping also, no doubt, that by presenting his niece to the New York public he might have a part of the golden harvest which he saw the Italian troupe was reaping.

Opposition, however, on the part of the Austrian authorities, in regard to issuing passports until Agostino could deposit a certain sum sufficient to provide for the rest of his family during his absence, had delayed their departure. In vain Lorenzo had recurred to his Muse and addressed a long *canzone* to Emperor Francis I, beseeching his personal intervention. Only when he was able to send four hundred and twenty dollars to his brother, was the latter allowed to sail from Austrian territory.

[8] *New York Review and Athenaeum Magazine,* vol. i, pp. 156, 241, and 325.
[9] *Memorie,* vol. ii, p. 123. See also a letter Da Ponte wrote to Alessandro Torri on April 29th, 1830, in Bernardi, *L. Da Ponte,* p. 202.

The meeting of the octogenarian Poet with his brother must have been touching.

"Asking and answering each other's questions," he relates in his *Memorie,* the last volume of which was published in that year, together with a modified reprint of the preceding ones,[10] "now in laughter, now in tears, we spent the remainder of that day and a good part of the night with the rest of the family. Then, overcome by happiness, we embraced each other again and retired to our rooms. It took me several hours to fall asleep, but when I finally did sleep, all the things of which we had spoken during the day became mixed up in my fancy, and I spent the rest of that night with our good father, with my brothers and sisters, and my friends of Venice, Treviso, Ceneda and many other Italian cities. I do not remember ever having had more delightful dreams during the whole course of my life."

For Giulia, Da Ponte staged his *L'ape musicale,* and though the work itself failed to arouse any enthusiasm, the New York public received the singer with marked favor on that occasion and in three subsequent concerts.[11] If, however, Lorenzo had hoped to profit by his niece's talent, he was sorely disappointed; for the girl, after these recitals, did not reappear on the stage. In 1832 she married a certain G. Stafler and with him returned to Trieste without even bidding her uncle and benefactor good-bye.[12]

But this grief faded into insignificance before that which overtook the aged Poet when, in the same year, his faithful and devoted Nancy died. In a letter dated June 9th, 1832, he wrote thus to his old-time friend Colombo:

[10] Vol. ii, p. 124.
[11] *Memorie,* vol. ii, pp. 128-29.
[12] See letter by Da Ponte to Stafler, dated September 30th, 1832, in Bernardi, *L. Da Ponte,* p. 228.

"For two years it seems as though Fate has taken pleasure in my sorrow, and if I were to tell you all my miseries, I am certain that I would cause you to shed many tears, and you deserve joys rather than afflictions. I shall write you but of one, and even little of that: for the present I shall say nothing about the others, which you will be able to read, if you care to, in the last volume of my sad *Memorie*. That of which I intend to inform you, is the untimely and unexpected death of that angel-like woman whom you saw in London. You know that she was twenty years younger than I, that she was, or at least seemed to be, of a healthy and strong constitution, and that she was not subject to any weakness which could give any suspicion of such a misfortune. She was taken away from me in only six days, and what was and is my grief at her death, neither you could imagine, nor I describe."[13]

This grief prompted him to write, shortly afterward, a certain number of sonnets, some of which he sent to his friends in Italy. These he later published in New York in a booklet containing also a very short compendium of his life and a portrait of Nancy.

The last six years of the old Poet's career were embittered by his incessant struggle for a bare existence. After the abrupt departure of his niece Giulia, he entered into a partnership with the French tenor Montrésor, who brought a company from Europe for a season at the Richmond Hill Theatre; but after thirty-five performances, including *Cenerentola* and *L' Italiana in Algeri* by Rossini, Bellini's *Pirata* and *Elisa e Claudio* by Mercadante, the venture failed disastrously. Undismayed, Da Ponte allied himself with a certain Riva-Finoli, purposing to establish the Italian opera permanently in New York. To that end, he exerted all his energy in securing financial backing from promi-

[13] Bernardi, *L. Da Ponte*, p. 189.

nent citizens, and he actually succeeded in having a theatre—the Italian Opera House—erected at the corner of Church and Leonard streets.

The season opened on the evening of November 18th, 1833, and it was a great social event. From a diary of Philip Hone, who was mayor of New York from 1826 to 1827, we learn that the auditorium of the theatre was magnificently decorated, rivaling in luxury and good taste the foremost European playhouses, that the stage settings were gorgeous and the seats large and comfortable.[14]

Of the forty performances scheduled, only twenty-eight were given, besides fifteen additional ones in Philadelphia. They comprised: *La gazza ladra, Il barbiere di Siviglia, La donna del lago, Il Turco in Italia, Cenerentola* and *Matilde di Shabran* by Rossini, *Il matrimonio segreto* by Cimarosa, *Gli Arabi nelle Gallie* by Pacini, and an opera by Maestro Salvioli, who was the orchestra conductor.

But this time also, Lorenzo, who to the enterprise had devoted all his efforts and in it had risked his little savings, met with a new disappointment. His partner Riva-Finoli disappeared and he was left alone to extricate himself as best he could from the embarrassing situation.

With a broken heart he saw, the following year, his theatre pass into other hands. For one more year Italian opera was given there, again unsuccessfully. In 1835 the place remained closed, then it was sold to James Wallack, who reopened it with a dramatic company, and finally, after another year, the theatre was

---

[14] See the interesting article *Sulle traccie dell' opera italiana in America*, by Pasquale De Biasi, in *Il Carroccio*, New York, vol. vii, Nos. 5-6 (May-June, 1918).

destroyed by fire. Thus the magnificent dream of Lorenzo Da Ponte ended in a cloud of smoke.

As was his custom, he had recourse to his facile pen in bringing his troubles to the attention of the public. Already in 1833 he had published a pamphlet entitled *Storia della compagnia dell' opera italiana condotta da Giacomo Montrésor in America in Agosto dell' anno 1832*, to which a second part was appended, called *Storia incredibile ma vera*. In 1835 he published still another pamphlet, with the sarcastic title *Frottola per far ridere*, in which he set forth all his complaints in connection with the failure of his operatic venture with Riva-Finoli.

"I do not know," he says, "whether a good or evil genius inspired me to bring music here also. I had hoped that in doing so my name might become immortal. It was just the opposite. My name was given instead to scorn, calumny, indigence and oblivion! I sunk in this enterprise all I had saved for my decrepit days, and I was rewarded with ingratitude BY EVERYBODY!"

And that his pupils also had deserted him, appears from this other passage of the same pamphlet:

"Eighteen months have passed since I had a single pupil. I, the creator of the Italian language in America, the teacher of more than two thousand persons whose progress astounded Italy! I, the poet of Joseph II, the author of thirty-six dramas, the inspiration of Salieri, of Weigl, of Martini, of Winter and Mozart! After twenty-seven years of hard labor, I have no longer a pupil! Nearly ninety years old, I have no more bread in America!"

No less bitterness breathes through his letters to his friends in the old world. "If Fate had led me to France instead of America," he writes to one of them, "I would not now fear that my remains might become food for the dogs; I would have earned enough money to secure rest for my old body in the grave and preserve my fame against total oblivion."[15] And to another: "No wonder that they are surprised in France to know I am still among the living, for in truth what I have suffered for so many years, and am still suffering in America, would have sufficed to send me more than once to join the desperate souls in Hades."[16]

In 1835 also he published a poem in five cantos dedicated to his lifelong friend Colombo in which he gives vent to his grief.[17] Part of the poem was translated into English by himself,—quite an ambitious attempt, if one considers that these are the first English verses of a man nearly ninety years old. This circumstance, and also the fact that they further depict his despondent frame of mind, lend a peculiar interest to them. He begins:

> Yet to the hand which has those treasures given,
> Ye have refused the cymbals and the lyre;
> And from *his* brow the laurel crown have riven,
> Whose name has set the proudest stage on fire.
> Have suffered one by cursed envy driven,
> (One who, when thousands he had all bereaved
> And none were left, his very self deceived)
> To bar to him the temple he had striven
> With pain and toil to rear. Permitted rage
> To seize the little mercy that was meant
> And given by another, to assuage
> The sorrows of a life so nearly spent,
> That good men trembled, as with taunting scorn,
> (And hate, of malice and of envy born)
> By ruthless hands *that* old man's hair was torn.
> Nor will I now what I have borne declare,
> My bitter wrongs, the horrors of my fate,

---

[15] Bernardi, *L. Da Ponte*, p. 235.
[16] *Ibid.*, p. 79.
[17] The title of the poem was *Storia Americana, ossia Il Lamento di Lorenzo Da Ponte quasi nonagenario al nonagenario Michele Colombo.*

Through life those wrongs and horrors will I bear.
My death, what now I speak not, shall relate.
They shall declare who love the sacred NINE,
To whom I consecrate my heart and song,
They shall declare that sorrows have been mine,
And pain and silent suffering and wrong—
For this heaven's light is still to me divine,
Nor will I at the ills I bear repine.
Oh! why does reverence the right deny
To speak the names that struggle in my breast?
Those *cherished names* whose mem'ry can not die
Until this beating bosom is at rest.
Those names alone have had the power to dry
The struggling tear, and check the rising sigh.
When in the garden, beautiful and fair,[18]
The jasmine blossomed, planted by my care,
The vi'let, the narcissus, and the rose,
The lily, type of virtue and repose,
The stately tulip and the fleur-de-lis,
Adding their beauty to the scenery,
While flowers of fairest and of richest hue,
Upon the air their sweetest perfume threw—
Spring into freshened life at my command,
Planted and raised and cultured by my hand.
When to the marsh-born magpie and the crow,
That garden's gates were ope'd but shut to me,
Those names I loved sustained me in my woe,
Checked my despair and soothed my misery.
For *them* I suffered that dogs, wolves, and all
The beasts of prey upon my flesh should fall,
Drink the warm current from my bleeding heart,
And glutted, deaf to all my cries, depart.
For this I took and nurtured in my breast
A ravenous beast, more fierce than all the rest,
In form a dove, but of his plumage shorn
A dove he came at earliest dawn of morn;
I found him plumage—mark the change at night,
A serpent writhes, discovered to my sight,
Sucks the heart's fountain to the very lees,
Contemns, betrays, traduces me and flees.

---

[18] To explain these lines, it must be stated that Da Ponte had given flower nicknames to his girl pupils.

In the English preface to the poem it is stated that his intention had been to return to Italy to die, but that he had been dissuaded by a letter from an admiring benefactor (probably Clement C. Moore), inclosing fifty dollars. He concludes:

"I remain. I will try to be known through the testimony of persons worthy of belief. It is my intention to publish fifty letters from distinguished persons in Europe.[19] They are all precious to me for their contents and the names of those who wrote them; but the name of the benevolent AMERICAN DONOR is, to me, the gem of the collection, both from the moment in which it was written, and all it says. One such citizen ennobles any place. New York may boast of many such—with her will I leave my ashes, as I have given to her thirty years of my life. Perhaps those ashes will receive, even from the ill-disposed and the ungrateful, *Vano conforto di tardi sospiri.*"

At nine in the evening, on August 17th, 1838, Da Ponte died of old age, at his home, No. 91 Spring Street.[20]

---

[19] No doubt Da Ponte had in his possession letters from famous men. Unless they were destroyed, they must have fallen into the hands of persons unaware of their value, for, despite all efforts, the present writer has been unable to trace any of them.

[20] An interesting investigation made by Krehbiel (*Music and Manners*, p. 173) in the New York City directories, reveals that Da Ponte changed his dwelling place at least 13 times during his stay in that city. He lived at the following addresses: 1807, No. 29 Partition St.; 1808, the Bowery; 1810, No. 247 Duane St.; 1819, No. 54 Chapel St.; 1820, No. 17 Jay St.; 1821, No. 343 Greenwich St.; 1824, No. 51 Hudson St.; 1825, No. 92 Hudson St.; 1826, No. 206 Duane St.; 1827 and 1828, No. 390 Greenwich St.; 1829 to 1835, No. 342 Broadway with the book-store at No. 336 (then, as now, the numbers were in the vicinity of Catherine Lane); 1836 and 1837, No. 35 Dey St.; 1838, No. 91 Spring St., where he died. Very appropriately Krehbiel remarks that "if it is true that three movings are as bad as a fire, Da Ponte's local peregrinations might be cited as either cause or proof of his poverty."

LAST YEARS

To the very last he retained his keen mentality and naïve vanity, which had accompanied him throughout life. Shortly before his last illness, he published a highly praised metrical translation of a portion of Hillhouse's *Hadad*,[21] and his attending physician and friend, Dr. John W. Francis, relates that on the day preceding his death he composed for him "a series of verses in his native tongue, partly in tone of gratitude, and partly to evince to his friends that, though speech had nigh left him, his mind was still entire."

All of his biographers agree that he died in the Catholic faith, and a number of letters published by Marchesan[22] confirm this statement beyond doubt.

His funeral, though announced in the *Evening Post* of August 18th, 1838, for the afternoon of the following day, was held a day later. Probably, as Krehbiel remarks,[23] the first plans of the family were changed after some of the Poet's friends had expressed a desire to honor his memory.

Tuckerman, who was an eye-witness, says:

"The obsequies of Da Ponte were impressive. The funeral took place at noon of the 20th of August, 1838. Allegri's Miserere was performed over his remains at the Cathedral. The pall-bearers were his countryman, Maroncelli, the companion of Pellico's memorable imprisonment at Spielberg; his old friend, Clement C. Moore, and two eminent citizens—the Hon. Gulian C. Verplanck and Dr. Macneven. On the coffin was a laurel wreath, and before it, on the way from the church to the Roman cemetery in Second-avenue, whither he was borne—followed by a long train of mourners led by the

---

[21] Dr. J. W. Francis, in his *Old New York*, says that Hillhouse's work was rendered in Italian by Da Ponte, "beautifully" and "with scholastic fidelity." Tuckerman (*L. Da Ponte*) calls it "accurate."

[22] *L. Da Ponte*, pp. 167-76.

[23] *Music and Manners*, p. 184.

officiating priests and the attendant physician[24]—was carried a banner, and on its black ground was this inscription:[25]

> LAURENTIUS DA PONTE
> Italia.Natus.
> Litterarum. Reipublicae. et. Musis.
> Dilectissimus.
> Patriae. et. Concivium. Amantissimus.
> Christianae. Fidei. Cultor. Adsiduus.
> In. Pace. et. Consolatione. Justorum.
> XVII. die. Augusti. MDCCCXXXVIII.
> XC. Anno. Aetatis. Suae.
> Amplexu. Domini.
> Ascendit."

A diligent investigation to locate the grave of Da Ponte was made by Krehbiel in 1887. He personally inspected the old Roman Catholic cemetery at Eleventh Street, between Avenue A and First Avenue, where the Poet's remains had been interred, and of his inspection gives the following account:

"The place is overgrown with rank grass and weeds. There are no paths. Those who wish to read the inscriptions on the head-stones must stumble along as best they can; now over irregular hillocks, now into deep depressions half-filled with old boots, rusty tin cans, and other refuse. Many of the inscriptions have been obliterated by the action of the elements; some of the stones lie prone upon the ground (the bones which once they guarded having been removed, as the bright-eyed, fresh-faced, silver-haired old wife of the decrepit keeper ex-

---

[24] J. G. Wilson (*Life etc of Fitz-Greene Halleck*, p. 406) says: "Among the many attached friends who followed the nonagenarian to the grave was his former pupil, Fitz-Greene Halleck."

[25] The inscription, as here given, is the one recorded by another eyewitness of the funeral, Samuel Ward, in his *Sketch of the Life of L. D. P.* Tuckerman, and Krehbiel after him, reproduce it with several mistakes: *conciorum* instead of *concivium*, *lustrorum* for *justorum*, and MDCCCXXXIII in place of MDCCCXXXVIII.

plains), and in one place a large Ailantus tree in growing has taken up a stone half-way into itself. For hours I crossed and recrossed the decaying cemetery, scrutinizing carefully every inscription; but in vain. No headstone was found bearing the name of Da Ponte, and there are no records to identify the spot where, on August 20, 1838, his grave was dug."[26]

Nor could any light be shed upon the subject by Lorenzo's descendants, and the same author publishes part of a letter written to him by E. Ellery Anderson, Esq., in which, after acknowledging his inability to give the desired information, the writer advances the following explanation: "My judgment is that his remains were placed temporarily in some friend's vault, with the intention of erecting a formal monument at a later period, and that this matter has been overlooked or forgotten until all traces of the poet's remains have been lost."[27]

Although, after this, any attempt further to investigate the matter seemed futile, the present author felt interested to inspect the "decaying cemetery" so vividly described by Krehbiel. The passing years have wrought many changes in that neighborhood, and the block where the cemetery was, is now—except for a little Catholic church and a garage—a dreary open space which strangely contrasts with the bustling life of the thickly settled surroundings.[28]

[26] *Music and Manners*, pp. 162-63.
[27] *Ibid.*, p. 185.
[28] Having inquired how it was that, despite the congested conditions of the district, no buildings had been erected in that block, the author received the curious information that a strong prejudice existed in that neighborhood, notwithstanding the many differences in race and creed, against building on land which had formerly been consecrated ground. The man who had built the garage, it was pointed out, had gone into bankruptcy.

A conversation with one of the Fathers of the little church brought out the information that all the gravestones and remains which were in the old churchyard had been transferred to Calvary Cemetery; and after a careful investigation of the records of the latter place no trace of a head-stone bearing Da Ponte's name was found. Thus, by a strange coincidence, the bones of the old Poet met with the same sad destiny as those of Mozart, and he who so often expressed in his declining years the fear that he would be neglected by posterity, was denied even the hoped for

Vano conforto di tardi sospiri.

THE END

APPENDIX

I. LETTER TO AN UNKNOWN PERSON IN SUNBURY, PA.

NEW YORK, Nov. 7th, 1824.

My Dear Sir:

Really I was not able to write you last Sunday, as I had hoped to do, and one of the principal reasons was a sudden illness of my daughter which kept us in continual fear and anxiety. Thank Heaven, for the last three days she has been much better, and therefore I write you; if it is not a long letter, I hope that you will pardon me, considering that Sunday is the only day of leisure in which I can write to my many friends.

I am sorry indeed that Sunbury, Northumberland, Milton and some of those other towns cannot offer a living to a modest young man, who would be satisfied with little and who could be very useful in teaching Latin, Italian, French and perhaps Spanish. Last week I sent fifteen grammars, as many dictionaries and some Italian books to Mr. Patten, professor in Middlebury College, where the Italian language is much studied and where they have a fine library of classical works of our authors. I have sent a professor to Baltimore, another to Philadelphia, and I am very glad to see that American students find a source of delight and knowledge in our books. I would like, therefore, to see them disseminated also in the Pennsylvanian mountains, and I had hoped that you, so well versed in this very beautiful language, would have been able to help me in my undertaking. Frankly, it ought to have been easy: ten or twelve pupils willing to pay only $10 for a course of three months, would have been enough for a beginning. Who knows! Maybe, realizing that we are satisfied with so little, students may yet be found.

The work for beginners which you suggest, I believe

would prove very useful; unfortunately, I am so busy keeping my pot boiling, that, for the present at least, I could not find time to do it. There are, however, booklets of that kind and at the first opporutnity I shall send you some, which will, at least in part, answer your needs. Perhaps I myself shall have the pleasure of bringing them to you. My coming to Sunbury depends on many things; within eight days probably I shall know whether the affairs of my children will oblige me to make this trip, which for no other reason will be pleasant to me except that I shall see and embrace you.

I should like meanwhile to have you take the trouble of seeing Mr. Colman Hall and asking him whether he has received a letter from my son Lorenzo with an order to pay to me the balance due to him from the legacy of his aunt Niccolini, and whether I can hope that the note sent to him will be accepted and paid by him in due time. Lorenzo is now in Philadelphia where he intends to practice law; his needs for this beginning are great, and I have not only him to support, but also another son who is studying medicine in New York, a daughter who was obliged to leave her husband, a wife and myself! and all this at the age of 76 and only with the sweat of my brow, since what comes to Mrs. Da Ponte from her sister is not enough to pay the house rent. If you have found something interesting in the first three volumes of my memoirs, I believe you will find much more in the fourth. And in reading it you will say with Dante:

E se non piangi, di che pianger suoli?

I would also like that you should try to persuade him to finish matters according to the testament; that is, I would like him to collect the money from Grant, if not from others, that he should set aside a sum sufficient to yield an interest of $300 for my wife and $36 for Carlo, and that, should a balance remain, he should see the justice of sending it to me, at a time in which I am so much in need of it to finish the education of my children, and especially of the youngest. I hope that my dear Doctor will gladly take charge of all this, and I hope also that this will contribute in letting me see Sunbury again. If you have the occasion of seeing Mr.

FACSIMILE OF A LETTER BY LORENZO DA PONTE, DATED NOVEMBER 7, 1824.

APPENDIX 143

Greenow, have the kindness of greeting and thanking him in my name. Probably next week either I shall write you or embrace you. Believe me
Your sincere and cordial friend,
LORENZO DA PONTE.

II. LETTER FROM A. DE LAMARTINE

In a condensed form, Da Ponte's autobiography has appeared in French and German, while, strange as it may seem, there has been no English translation. The French translation, a work by M. C. D. de la Chevanne (Paris, Pagnerre, 1860), is preceded by a letter from Lamartine, quoted here as it shows what an exaggerated opinion the French poet had of Da Ponte's *Memorie*. It is curious to note that both La Chevanne and Lamartine give a French twist to our Poet's name and call him D' Aponte!

Mon cher La Chevanne,
Voici les Mémoires les plus originaux et les plus anecdotiques que l'Italie artiste ait jamais offerts à la curiosité publique.
Les Mémoires de Benvenuto Cellini ne sont ni plus naïfs, ni plus amusants. Le monde a quelquefois besoin de penser, mais il a quelquefois aussi besoin de s'amuser. Le plaisir honnête est une des quatre fins de l'homme. Traduisez donc pour le public français les Mémoires que je vous envoie ici; ce ne sera pas du temps perdu. Tout le monde lira et sourira.
L' auteur est un Vénitien, du temps où les Vénitiens étaient le peuple le plus spirituel et le plus aimable de ce bal masqué en permanence qu'on appelait Venise. Depuis, ils sont devenus des victimes de la politique. Livrés par nos mains, hélas! à l'Autriche, plus tard ils sont devenus des héros malheureux, auxquels nous voudrions tendre la main, si cette main était assez longue, à travers leurs lagunes; ils ont produit Manin, l'infortuné Washington d'un jour! Ils n'en sont que plus intéressants. On aime à remonter aux jours heureux de leur histoire. Voici un homme qui vous y reportera.
Il se nomme D'Aponte [*sic*]. Il passa sa jeunesse à aimer, à chanter des barcarolles, à intriguer en masque sur la place de Saint-Marc, comme toute sa patrie; plus tard il connut l' immortel Mozart, ce Rossini de son

siècle, aussi gai, mais plus sensible et plus spiritualiste que le Rossini de notre âge. Il se dévoua par enthousiasme pour la musique à ce Raphaël de la mélodie, Mozart; il donna un corps à toutes ces notes auxquelles Mozart donnait l'âme. Il fut l'ombre inséparable de ce grand homme. N'est-ce pas quelque chose? Mozart et D'Aponte étaient amis; un grand compositeur, en ce temps-là, ne dédaignait pas d'aimer un grand poëte. Les arts étaient égaux, les cœurs aussi; ce n'était pas apparemment comme de nos jours.

D'Aponte est, dans ses Mémoires, aussi écrivain que Goldoni, son compatriote, aussi léger que le chevalier de Grammont, aussi aventureux que Gil Blas, aussi plaisant que Figaro, aussi malheureux que Gilbert. Combien de titres pour réussir après sa mort! Ressuscitez cet homme enseveli mal à propos. Ses Mémoires introuvables étaient enfouis dans cette forêt d'Amérique qu'on appelle New York. Personne ne les aurait exhumés là-bas, où le plus ingénieux manuscrit ne pèsera jamais le poids d'un dollar. J'en dois la première communication à ce musicien passionné et à cet écrivain exquis qu'on appelle à Paris Scudo. Scudo seul était digne d'être le dépositaire de ce trésor; les notes, pour lui, sont des mots, et les mots sont des notes. Il traduit le son en pensée et la pensée en son. Ne l'avez-vous pas vu quelquefois à l'opéra italien pendant qu'on jouait Mozart ou Cimarosa? Je l'ai vu hier encore, moi, debout entre deux colonnes, élevant ses deux mains en conque à ses oreilles, comme pour mieux boire le vent de l'orchestre, et tournant son visage pâli contre les parois de la loge, comme pour cacher au public la pudeur et l'excès de ses émotions musicales. Cette oreille de Scudo est si fine, qu'elle discernerait et qu'elle noterait une mélodie dans les frissons d'une brise d'été à travers des brins de gazon. Remerciez-le, faites comme lui, et vous ferez bien; remerciez surtout M. de Saint-Hilaire, autre dilettante exquis capable d'interpréter Mozart et d'aimer D'Aponte. C'est à lui que je dois le rare exemplaire de ces mémoires que je vous confie. Je vous promets un monde choisi de lecteurs qui se renouvelleront avec les années; je vous donne un certificat de succès et de plaisir pour votre jeune éditeur, M. Pagnerre. Puisse ce certificat bien sincère vous porter bonheur à tous deux, et que l' ombre mélodieuse de Mozart, et que l'ombre capricieuse de D'Aponte vous soient en aide ! Adieu et amitié.

AL. DE LAMARTINE.

Paris, 20 juillet 1860.

BIBLIOGRAPHY

I. Principal Works of L. Da Ponte

A. *LYRIC*

1. *Accademia poetica.* Recited in the Seminary of Treviso at the close of the academic year 1775-76, published for the first time by Angelo Marchesan in his "Della vita e delle opere di Lorenzo Da Ponte," Treviso, Tip. Turazza, 1900.
2. *Il capriccio. La gratitudine o sia la difesa delle donne.* Gorizia, 1780. They were later reprinted in the *Saggi Poetici.*
3. *Versi sciolti a S. E. Giorgio Pisani.* In "Poesie per il solene ingresso di S. Ecc. Mss. Zorzi Pisani, Procuratore di S. Marco per merito." Venice, 1781.
4. *Saggi poetici dell' ab. L. Da Ponte, poeta al servizio di Sua Maestà Cesarea.* Vol. i, dedicated to Prince Ludwig von Batthyani-Strattmann; vol. ii, dedicated to Count Franz Kohary. Vienna, Imp. stamperia dei sordi e muti, 1788.
5. *Il tributo del core, poesie di Lorenzo Da Ponte.* London, printed by M. Stace, 1793.
6. *La profezia di Dante* [Byron's] *tradotta in terza rima da L. Da Ponte.* New York, printed by R. & W. A. Bartow, 1821. It was reprinted a year later by the same firm with notes and some additional poems. Afterwards it was included in the last volume of the *Memorie.* Bernardi also republished it in his "Memorie compendiate di L. Da Ponte," Florence, Le Monnier, 1871.
7. *Poesie varie,* second edition. New York, printed by John Turney, 1830. It is a reprint of the second part of Vol. iii of the *Memorie,* with some other poems appended.

8. *Alcune poesie di Lorenzo Da Ponte pubblicate da lui medesimo in New York l' anno 1830*. This booklet, of only 31 pages, had other titles also, among which those of *Mazzetti di fiori* and *Mazzetti di fiori austriaci*.
9. *Sonetti per la morte di Anna Celestina Ernestina Da Ponte*. New York, 1832. The booklet, containing also a portrait of the author and one of his wife, is preceded by a compendium of the *Memorie* made by Da Ponte himself.
10. *Storia americana ossia Il Lamento di Lorenzo Da Ponte quasi nonagenario al nonagenario Michele Colombo*. New York, 1835.
11. A translation into Italian verse of part of Hillhouse's "Hadad."

B. DRAMATIC

12. ...., a tragedy translated from German (?), produced in Gorizia in 1779 or 1780 (*Memorie*, vol. i, p. 73).
13. *Il conte di Warwick* (1777-79), a tragedy by J. F. de La Harpe, translated from French in collaboration with Girolamo Da Ponte, and recited in Gorizia in 1779 or 1780 (*Mem.* vol. i, p. 73).
14. *Il ricco d' un giorno* (1783-84), a libretto in three acts set to music by Antonio Salieri and performed at the Court Theatre of Vienna during the autumn of 1784 (*Mem.* vol. i, pp. 97-102).
15. *Il burbero di buon cuore* (1785), a libretto in three acts, derived from Goldoni's *Bourru bienfaisant*, and set to music by Vicente Martin y Solar. It was given at the Court Theatre of Vienna on Jan. 4th, 1786 (*Mem.* vol. i, pp. 106-7).
16. *Il finto cieco* (1785 or 1786), an adaptation of an older libretto, music by Giuseppe Gazzaniga, performed at the Court Theatre in Vienna, in 1786 (*Mem.* vol. i, p. 110).
17. *Le nozze di Figaro* (1786), a libretto derived from Beaumarchais' *Mariage de Figaro*, set to music by W. A. Mozart, and given for the first time at the Vienna Court Theatre, on May 1st, 1786 (*Mem.* vol. i, pp. 110-11 and 118-20). The ms. is in the Imperial Library of the Court, in Vienna—Tab. cod. Vol. ix, p. 177, No. 16,566. This libretto was translated into other languages countless times.

18. *Gli equivoci* (1786), an adaptation from Shakespeare's *Comedy of Errors*, music by Stefano Storace, presented at the Court Theatre, in Vienna, in 1786 (*Mem.* vol. i, p. 124).

19. *Una cosa rara o sia bellezza ed onestà* (1786), a libretto derived from *La luna de la Sierra* by Luis Velez de Guevara, set to music by Vicente Martin, and produced at the Vienna Court Theatre during the autumn of 1786 (*Mem.* vol. i, pp. 124-28). The ms. is in the Imperial Library of the Court, in Vienna—Tab. cod. Vol. x, p. 61, No. 17,794.

20. *Il Demogorgone o sia il filosofo confuso* (1786), music by Vincenzo Righini, given at the Vienna Court Theatre during the autumn of 1786 (*Mem.* vol. i, p. 129).

21. *Bertoldo* (1787), an adaptation of an old libretto by Brunati, set to music by Francesco Piticchio, and given in Vienna (Court Theatre) from June 22d to August 5th, 1787 (*Mem.* vol. i, p. 130).

22. *L' arbore di Diana* (1787), a libretto in two acts, music by Vicente Martin, produced at the Vienna Court Theatre, on October 1st, 1787 (*Mem.* vol. i, pp. 130-33). The ms. is in the Imperial Library of the Court, in Vienna—Tab. cod. Vol. x, p. 61, No. 17,795. It was published in 1788, in Vienna (J. Kurzbek, printer), and republished in Padua, in 1827 (Tip. Penada). There is a German translation of this libretto.

23. *Il dissoluto punito o sia il Don Giovanni* (1787), an adaptation from an older libretto by Giovanni Bertati, set to music by W. A. Mozart, given for the first time in Prague, on October 29th, 1787, and repeated, with slight changes, in Vienna (Court Theatre), on May 7th, 1788 (*Mem.* vol. i, pp. 133-35). Of this work there are countless translations in many languages.

24. *Axur, re d'Ormus* (1787), an adaptation from Beaumarchais' *Tarare*, music by Antonio Salieri, produced at the Court Theatre, in Vienna, on January 8th, 1788 (*Mem.* vol. i, p. 134). The ms. is in the Imperial Library of the Court, in Vienna—Tab. cod. Vol. x, p. 65, No. 17,832. It was printed in Vienna by J. Kurzbek, in 1788.

25. *Il talismano* (1788), an adaptation from Goldoni's play by the same title, set to music by Antonio Salieri, and presented at the Vienna Court Theatre in 1788. The ms. is in the Imperial Library of the Court, in Vienna —Tab. cod. Vol. ix, p. 182, No. 16,604. There is no mention of this work in the *Memorie*.

26. *Il pastor fido* (1788 or 1789), probably an adaptation from an older libretto, set to music by Antonio Salieri, and produced at the Court Theatre, in Vienna, on Feb. 11th, 1789 (*Mem.* vol. i, p. 139).

27. *Il pasticcio o l' ape musicale* (1789), a musical "revue" introducing the most popular selections from operas recently given in Vienna. It was presented at the Vienna Court Theatre, in the Lenten season of 1789, then again in Trieste (1791), and finally in New York, in the spring of 1830 (*Mem.* vol. i, pp. 139 and 161; vol. ii, pp. 128-29).

28. *La cifra* (1789), an adaptation from another libretto, *La dama pastorella*, by Romano Petrosolini. It was set to music by Antonio Salieri, and produced in Vienna (Court Theatre) on December 11th, 1789 (*Mem.* vol. i, p. 138). The ms. is in the Imperial Library of the Court, in Vienna—Tab. cod. Vol. ix, p. 177, No. 16,566.

29. *Così fan tutte o la scuola delle amanti* (1789), a libretto set to music by W. A. Mozart, and given at the Vienna Court Theatre, on January 26th, 1790 (*Mem.* vol. i, p. 139). There are many translations of this work.

30. *Il tempio di Flora o Flora e Minerva* (1790 or 1791), a cantata, with music by Joseph Weigl. It was presented in Vienna, at the little private theatre of Prince Adam von Auesperg, Jan. 17th, 1791 (*Mem.* vol. i, pp. 141-42).

31. *I voti della nazione napoletana* (1790 or 1791), a cantata, with music by Francesco Piticchio, produced at the palace of the Neapolitan Embassy in Vienna, in January, 1791 (*Mem.* vol. i, pp. 143-44).

32. *Davide* (1791), an oratorio in four parts, music by (?), prepared for performance at the Vienna Court Theatre during Lent of 1791. It is not known whether it was ever actually given (*Mem.* vol. i, p. 147).

33. *Il Mezenzio* (1791), a tragedy, presented for the first time at the Imperial and Royal Theatre, in Trieste, during

the autumn of 1791 (*Mem.* vol. i, p. 161). This tragedy was published in New York (Joseph Desnones, Printer, 1834), together with *Le nozze di Figaro, Don Giovanni* and *Axur, re d' Ormus*. A libretto derived from it was presented by Da Ponte to the singer Gertrude Elizabeth Schmoelling Mara, in London. It is not known whether it was ever set to music (*Mem.* vol. i, p. 187).[1]

34. *La morte di Luigi XVI* [?] (1793), a drama begun in London and probably never finished. See Nicolini's notes to the *Memorie*, vol. ii, p. 296.
35. *Le lagrime della regina di Francia* (1793), an aria with chorus. See Nicolini's notes to the *Memorie*, vol. ii, p. 296.
36. .... (1793), a play prepared for the announced arrival of Emperor Francis in Holland, probably never finished. See Nicolini's notes to the *Memorie*, vol. ii, p. 298.
37. .... (1793), a cantata written on occasion of the recovery of the Prince of Orange. It was neither set to music, nor printed. See Nicolini's notes to the *Memorie*, vol. ii, p. 298.
38. *La scuola de' maritati* (1794), a libretto, a severe criticism of which was anonymously published, in a scurrilous pamphlet by the Poet's rival, Carlo Francesco Badini.[2] See p. 92.
39. *La capricciosa corretta* (1794), a libretto in two acts, set to music by Vicente Martin, and presented at the Drury Lane Theatre in London, in 1794 or 1795 (*Mem.* vol. i, pp. 198-200).
40. *L' isola del piacere* (1794 or 1795), a libretto with music by Vicente Martin, produced at the Drury Lane Theatre in London, in 1795 (*Mem.* vol. i, pp. 198-200).
41. *Merope* (1795?), a libretto set to music by Francesco Bianchi and produced at the Drury Lane Theatre in London, in 1799 (*Mem.* vol. i, pp. 196 and 200).

[1] This tragedy is not mentioned by Marchesan, nor by Nicolini. Evidently the existence of the New York edition was unknown to them.
[2] This libretto also is unmentioned by either Marchesan or Nicolini.

42. .... (1795), a cantata for the wedding of the Prince of Wales with Elizabeth of Brunswick. It is not known by whom it was set to music. It was presented later, in London, on occasion of "a victory" (*Mem.* vol. i, p. 207).
43. *Semira e Azor* (between 1795 and 1798), a translation of the libretto *Zémyre et Azor*, set to music by Grétry. It was given at the Drury Lane Theatre in one of the mentioned years (*Mem.* vol. i, pp. 201-3).
44. *Evelina* (between 1795 and 1798), a translation of *Arvire et Eveline*, with music by Sacchini and Rey, presented at Drury Lane Theatre in one of the mentioned years (*Mem.* vol. i, p. 207).
45. *Armida* (1803 or 1804), a one act farce with music by Peter Winter, given at the Drury Lane Theatre in 1804 (*Mem.* vol. i, p. 207).
46. *Castore e Polluce o il trionfo dell' amor fraterno* (1803), a libretto set to music by Peter Winter and presented at the Drury Lane Theatre in 1803 (*Mem.* vol. i, p. 254).
47. *Il ratto di Proserpina* (1804), a libretto with music by Peter Winter. It was produced at the Drury Lane Theatre in 1804 (*Mem.* vol. i, p. 254).

C. PROSE

48. *Storia compendiosa della vita di Lorenzo Da Ponte, scritta da lui medesimo. A cui si aggiunge la prima letteraria conversazione tenuta in sua casa, il giorno 10 marzo dell' anno 1807, in New York, consistente in alcune composizioni italiane, si in verso che in prosa, tradotte in inglese dai suoi allievi* ("Compendium of the Life of Lorenzo Da Ponte, written by Himself, to which is added the first Literary Conversazione held at His House in New York on the 10th day of March 1807, consisting of several Italian compositions in verse and prose, translated into English by his scholars"). New York, printed by I. Riley & Co., 1807.
49. *Sull' Italia. Discorso apologetico in riposta alla lettera dell' avvocato Phillips.* New York, 1821. An English translation of it was published at the same time.
50. *Catalogo ragionato de' libri che si trovano al negozio di Lorenzo e Carlo Da Ponte.* New York, 1823.

51. *Alcune osservazioni sull' articolo quarto pubblicato nel "North American Review" il mese d' ottobre dell' anno 1824.* New York, printed by Gray & Bunce, 1825.
52. *Critique on certain passages in Dante.* A series of articles which appeared in 1825 in the "New York Review and Athenaeum Magazine", vol. i, pp. 156-58, 241-42 and 325-27. They were republished by T. Koch in the Appendix to the "Fifteenth Annual Report of the Dante Society", Boston, May 1896.
53. *Memorie di Lorenzo Da Ponte da Ceneda scritte da esso*, published by Lorenzo and Carlo Da Ponte. New York, John Gray & Co., Printers, 1823-26-27. In four little volumes.
54. *Storia della lingua e letteratura italiana in New York. Con alcune lettere italiane, francesi e spagnole delle damigelle della sua triplice classe. E due lettere ad rem del sig. E. Mathias all' autore.* New York, printed by Gray & Bunce, 1827.
55. *Memorie di Lorenzo Da Ponte da Ceneda scritte da esso. Seconda edizione corretta e ampliata con note dell' autore e l' aggiunta d'un volume.* New York; in three volumes, the first two of which were printed in 1829, by Gray & Bunce; the third, in 1830, by John Turney. Each volume is divided in two parts: part i of vol. i is of 86 pages; part ii, of 159,—part i of vol. ii is of 148 pages; part ii, of 108,—part i of vol. iii is of 127 pages; part ii (containing poems by the author), of 132.

    This work, which had become a real rarity, was recently republished in Italy in two very accurate editions: one, in one volume, with an introduction by Serafino Paggi, was edited in Ferdinando Martini's collection, "Classici Italiani" (Milan, 1916); the other, in two volumes, was edited by G. Gambarin and F. Nicolini, in the Laterza collection, "Scrittori d' Italia" (Bari, 1918). The latter edition, undoubtedly the better, and the one to which reference has been made throughout this work, besides having very interesting appendices, contains exhaustive and scholarly notes by F. Nicolini.

    For existing translations of the *Memorie,* see Appendix, II.
56. *Storia della compagnia dell' opera italiana condotta da Giacomo Montrésor in America in Agosto dell' anno 1832*—and *Storia incredibile ma vera.* New York, printed by Joseph Desnones, 1833.
57. *Frottola per far ridere—dedicata all' illustre sig. B. Gamba.* New York, 1835.

II. WORKS ABOUT L. DA PONTE

A. IN ITALIAN

58. MONICO, GIUSEPPE. *Il Cecchino, novella poetica di Lorenzo Da Ponte.* Treviso, 1819. The preface contains some biographical notes on the poet.
59. MONTANI. *Antologia,* vol. xxx, Nos. 88-89. Florence, 1828.
60. TORRI, ALESSANDO. *Nuovo Giornale dei letterati,* No. 102, November 1838.
61. GAMBA, BARTOLOMEO. *Biografia di Lorenzo Da Ponte,*—an article in *Biografia degli italiani illustri nelle scienze, lettere ed arti del sec. XVIII e de' contemporanei, compilata da letterati italiani di ogni provincia e pubblicata a cura del Prof. Emilio De Tipaldo,* vol. viii, p. 256. Venice, 1841.
62. BERNARDI, JACOPO. *Memorie di Lorenzo Da Ponte compendiate da Jacopo Bernardi, e scritti vari in prosa e poesia del medesimo autore.* Florence, Le Monnier, 1871.
63. MASI, ERNESTO. *Studi e ritratti.* Bologna, Tip. Nic. Zanichelli, 1881.
64. DE MARCHI, EMILIO. *Lettere e letterati italiani del secolo XVIII.* Milan, Tip. Briola, 1882.
65. TROYER, F. *Note storiche su Vittorio,* in *Le cento città, d'Italia,* a monthly supplement to *Il Secolo* of Milan. Vol. vii, No. 75, March 23d, 1893.
66. CENTELLI, ATTILIO. *Gli avventurieri della letteratura. Lorenzo Da Ponte,* in *Natura ed Arte.* Milan, Tip. Vallardi, vol. ii, No. 21, October 1st, 1893.
67. MARSON, LUIGI. *Guida di Vittorio e suo distretto. Cenni storici,* p. 98. Treviso, Tip. Zoppelli.
68. GIURATI, DOMENICO. *Su Lorenzo Da Ponte a proposito del Don Giovanni,* in *Illustrazione italiana.* Milan, Treves, vol. xxiv, No. 2, January 10th, 1897.
69. BONI, GIACOMO. *Studi danteschi in America,* in *Rivista d' Italia.* Rome, Società Editrice Dante Alighieri, June 15th, 1898.
70. LOZZI, CESARE. *Due abati del settecento inspiratori di melodrammi famosi,* in *Gazzetta Musicale di Milano.* Milan, Giulio Ricordi, vol. liv, No. 32, August 10th, 1899.

71. CONCARI, TULLO. *Il Settecento*, in *Storia letteraria d'Italia, scritta da una società di professori*. Milan, Tip. Fr. Vallardi, 1898-1900.
72. MAZZONI, GUIDO. *L' ottocento*, also in *Storia letteraria d' Italia*, etc. Milan, Tip. Fr. Vallardi, 1898-1900.
73. MARCHESAN, ANGELO. *Della vita e delle opere di Lorenzo Da Ponte*. Treviso, Tip. Turazza, 1900.
74. MAZZONI, GUIDO. An article in *Rivista d'Italia*, 1900.
75. NOVATI, F. *A ricolta, studi e profili*. Bergamo, 1907.
76. RAVA, ALDO. *Un' operetta sconosciuta sulla morte di Luigi XVI*, in *Marzocco*. Florence, June 25th, 1911.
77. RAVA, ALDO. *Lettere di donne a G. Casanova*. Milan, Treves, 1912.
78. PAGGI, SERAFINO. *Lorenzo Da Ponte*,—an introduction to the *Memorie*, in the Martini edition. Milan, Istituto Editoriale Italiano, 1916.
79. MOLMENTI, POMPEO. *Carteggi Casanoviani*. Vol. i, "Lettere di G. Casanova e di altri a lui"—Vol. ii, "Lettere del patrizio Zaguri a G. Casanova." Palermo, Remo Sandron, 1916 and 1918.
80. NICOLINI, FAUSTO. Notes to the *Memorie*, as edited by him and G. Gambarin. Bari, Gius. Laterza & Figli, 1918.
81. DE BIASI, PASQUALE. *Sulle traccie dell' opera italiana in America*, in *Il Carroccio*. New York, vol. vii, Nos. 5-6 (May-June, 1918).

B. IN ENGLISH

82. KELLY, MICHAEL. *Reminiscences*. Second edition. London, 1826.
83. WARD, SAMUEL. *Sketch on the Life of Lorenzo Da Ponte of Ceneda*. It was first published in the *New York Mirror* (August 1838), then in pamphlet form (1842).
84. FRANCIS, JOHN W. *Old New York*. New York, W. J. Widdleton, 1866.
85. TUCKERMAN, HENRY T. *Lorenzo Da Ponte*,—an article which first appeared in *Putnam's Magazine* (vol. xii, pp. 527-36, November 1868), later in the *Dublin University Magazine* (vol. lxxx, pp. 215-24, August 1872). A French translation of it was published in the *Revue Britannique*.

86. KREHBIEL, HENRY E. *Da Ponte in New York,*—an essay which was first published in the *New York Tribune* (August 28th, 1887), and later was included in the following works by the same author: *Review of the New York Musical Season 1889-90* and *Music and Manners in the Classical Period.* New York, Scribner, 1898.
87. ROSS, JANET. *Mozart's Librettist* in *Macmillan's Magazine*, vol. lxv, pp. 53-56, November 1891.
88. CARPENTER, GEORGE RICE. *Lorenzo Da Ponte*, in *Columbia Literary Monthly*, vol. iii, pp. 289-92, April 1895.
89. KOCH, THEODORE W. *Dante in America, A Historical and Bibliographical Study*, in the *Fifteenth Annual Report of the Dante Society*, May 19th, 1896. Boston, Ginn & Co., 1896.
90. MACKINLAY, M. S. *Garcia the Centenarian and His Times.* London, W. Blackwood & Sons, 1908.
91. DENT, EDWARD J. *Mozart's Operas.* London, Chatto & Windus, 1913.
92. LITTLEFIELD, WALTER. An article in *The New York Times*, spring 1915.
93. GOGGIO, EMILIO. An article in the *Romanic Review*, vol. x, pp. 259-261, 1919.
94. *Autolycus.* A short article in *The Athenaeum* of April 2d, 1920.
95. PORTERFIELD, ALLEN WILSON. An article in the New York *Evening Post* of October 29th, 1921.
96. ALDRICH, RICHARD. An article in *The New York Times* of March 19th, 1922.
97. LITTLEFIELD, WALTER. An article in *The New York Times* of April 2d, 1922.
98. KREHBIEL, HENRY E. An article in the *New York Tribune* of April 9th, 1922.
99. LITTLEFIELD, WALTER. An article in the *New York Tribune* of April 16th, 1922.
100. RUSSO, JOSEPH LOUIS. An article in *The New York Times* of April 23d, 1922.
101. KREHBIEL, HENRY E. An article in the *New York Tribune* of April 23d, 1922.

C. IN FRENCH

102. LAMARTINE, ALPHONSE DE. *Cours familier de Littérature*, vol. v, p. 406 *et seq*. Paris, 1858. This article was reproduced as an introduction to the French translation of the *Memorie* made by La Chevanne.

D. IN GERMAN

103. .... *Lorenzo Da Ponte als Wiener Theaterdichter*, in *Sammel-Bände der Internat. Musikgesellschaft, 15. Jahrg.*
104. MEISSNER, ALFRED. See his *Kulturbilder*.
105. LANDAU, MARKUS. *La letteratura italiana alla corte d'Austria*. First Italian translation. Aquila, Tip. R. Grossi, 1880.
106. LÖHNER, E. VON. *Lorenzo Da Ponte*, in the *Wiener Zeitung*, 1884.
107. .... An article in the *Wiener Fremdenblatt*, 1899.

NOTE

Besides the works listed above, almost every biography of Mozart contains some passages on Da Ponte.

Short notices on him are found in almost every encyclopaedia; fairly good articles, in *The Catholic Encyclopedia*, in Larousse's *Grand Dictionnaire Universel*, in Meyer's *Konversations-Lexikon*, as well as in the following works: Brockhous, Appleton's *Cyclopaedia of American Biography*, Duyckinck's *Cyclopaedia of American Literature*, *The Cambridge History of American Literature*, *U. S. Catholic Historical Society, Hist. Records and Studies* (vol. v, part i), and *Allgemeine Deutsche Biographie*.

Finally, it may not be out of place to mention that a novel also was written on our Poet: *Daponte* [sic] *und Mozart*, by Julius Grosse, Jena, 1874.

INDEX

The heavy type indicates authors to whom reference has been made.

Académie de Dijon, 23.
Accademia dei Granelleschi, 15.
Accademia dei Solleciti, 21 f.
Accademia dell'Arcadia, cf. Arcadia.
Accademia given by D. P. in Treviso, 23-32.
Albertarelli, singer, 70.
Albrechtsberger, 72 f.
Alcune osservazioni sull'articolo quarto, etc., 120 f.
Aleardi, Aleardo, 25.
Alighieri, cf. Dante.
Allegranti, Maddelena, singer, 98.
Altanesi, Giovan Francesco, 33.
Anafesto, Paolo Lucio, Venetian Doge, 12 f.
Anderson, Elbert Ellery, 118 f., 139.
Anderson family, 118 f.
Anderson, Henry James, son-in-law of D. P., 117, 118.
Angrisani, singer, 126.
Anthony, Prince of Saxony, 68.
Antonioli, librettist, 85.
Attems family, 43.
Ape musicale (L'), cf. Pasticcio.
Arbore di Diana (L'), 55 f., 65-68.
Arcadia, 22 f., 44.
Aremberg family, 87.
Ariosto, 4, 99 f., 120 f.
Axur, re d'Ormus, 49 f., 65, 66, 69, 70.

Bachi, Pietro, XI.
Badini, Carlo Francesco, librettist, 85-89, 92.
Balbi, Paolo, 14.
Banti, Brigida Giorgi, singer, 89, 90, 93-95, 98, 100, 102.
Barbieri, Signora, singer, 126, 128.
Bassano, painters, 1.
Beaumarchais' *Mariage de Figaro,* 60, 61; *Tarare,* 66.
Bedford, Duke of, 86 f.
Beethoven, XII, 49 f.
Bellaudi, Angioletta, 39, 40, 97.
Bellini, Vincenzo, 131.
Benucci, singer, 63, 70.
Bériot, Charles de, 126 f.
Bernardi, Jacopo, XIII, *Memorie di L. D. P. compendiate,* 4 f., 5 f., 6 f., 7 f., 8 f., 9 f., 13 f., 17 f., 19 f., 22 f., 69 f., 71 f., 104 f., 129 f., 130 f., 131 f., 134 f.
Berni, Francesco, 29, 120 f.
Bertati, Giovanni, librettist, 67.
Bertoldo, 65.
Bianchi, Francesco, composer, 89, 90.
Bible, 48.
Bologna, 97, 98.
Bonaparte, Joseph, 126, 127.
Bonaparte, Napoleon, cf. Napoleon.
Brander, Virginia, 116 f.
Brigido, Count Pompeo Benvenuto, 77, 79, 80.
Brussels, 87.

INDEX

Bujer family, 112.
Burbero di buon cuore (Il), 55 f., 56.
Businello, 10 f.
Bussani, singer, 63.
Byron, XII, 119.

Cagliari, Abbé, 3.
Calderon, 64.
Cantata on the occasion of the wedding of George IV with Elizabeth of Brunswick, 94.
Canzone in morte di Giuseppe II, 72.
Capriccio (Il), 44.
Capricciosa corretta (La), 90, 91.
Caroline, Queen of England, 117.
Carpenter, George R., XVII.
Casanova, Giacomo, XIII, XVII, 33, 83-88; *Mémoires*, 10, 11; *Carteggi Casanoviani*, 31 f., 36, 37, 75 f., 76, 77 f., 80 f., 82 f., 84, 85, 88, 91, 93.
Casti, Giambattista, 52 f., 53-58, 62-64, 80, 101.
Castore e Polluce o Il trionfo dell'amor fraterno, 102.
Catalogo ragionato de' libri, etc., 119.
Catherine II of Russia, 33 f.
Cavalieri, Signora, singer, 70.
Cecchino (Il), 22.
Ceneda, 1-6, 19, 40, 52 f., 94-97, 130; Bishop of, cf. Da Ponte, Lorenzo; Seminary of, 3-6.
Centelli, Attilio, XV; *Gli avventurieri della letteratura. Lorenzo Da Ponte*, 2 f., 31 f., 47 f.
Cesarotti, Melchiorre, 35.
Cherubini, 49 f., 94 f.
Cifra (La), 71.
Cimarosa, 132.
Cobenzl, Count Guido von, 43. 46.
Cobenzl, Count Johann Philipp von, 43, 46.
Collalto, Count de, 80 f.
Colletti, Giuseppe de, 44-46.
Colombo, Michele, 4, 6, 8, 9, 13, 17-19, 101, 104, 130, 131, 134.
Colonia Sonziaca, 44.
Columbia University, XI, XVII, 110 f., 111 f., 115, 118, 120-24.
Compendium of the Life, etc., 109, 111.
Conclusione degli studi, 8, 23, 24.
Conegliano, Geremia, cf. Da Ponte, Gaspare.
Cooper, Fenimore, 127.
Coronini, Count Rodolfo, 43.
Cosa rara (Una), 55 f., 64, 65, 80, 108.
Cosi fan tutte o La scuola delle amanti, XI, 71, 92 f.
Crivelli, singer, 126.
Croce, Benedetto, 33 f.
Crotta, Sebastiano, 14.

Da Lezze, Giovanni, 75.
Dal Pozzo, Pietro, 85.
Damiani, Natale, singer, 98.
Dante, XI, XVII, 4, 65, 119, 129.
Da Ponte, Agostino, Lorenzo's half-brother, 76, 129, 130.
Da Ponte, Anna Celestina Ernestina, Lorenzo's wife, 78 f., 79, 81-85, 87, 88, 93, 95-98, 103, 104, 107, 108, 109, 112, 113, 115, 118, 130, 131.
Da Ponte, Carlo, Lorenzo's son, 105, 115, 119, 120.
Da Ponte, Durant, Lorenzo's grandson, 105 f.
Da Ponte, Enrico, Lorenzo's great-grandson, 105 f.
Da Ponte, Fanny, Lorenzo's daughter, 105, 118.
Da Ponte, Faustina, Lorenzo's half-sister, 96.
Da Ponte, Francesco (Bassano), 1.

Da Ponte, Gaspare, Lorenzo's father, 2, 3, 49, 52, 95, 96, 130.
Da Ponte, Giambattista (Bassano), 1.
Da Ponte, Giovanni Antonio, 1.
Da Ponte, Girolamo, Lorenzo's brother, 2, 3, 5, 6, 18, 19, 21-23, 33, 52.
Da Ponte, Girolamo (Bassano), 1.
Da Ponte, Giulia, Lorenzo's niece, 129-31.
Da Ponte, Giuseppe, Lorenzo's son, 104, 114-16.
Da Ponte, Jacopo (Bassano), 1.
Da Ponte, Leandro (Bassano), 1.
Da Ponte, Lorenzo, Bishop of Ceneda, 2, 3, 6.
Da Ponte, Lorenzo, Lorenzo's great-grandson, 105 f.
Da Ponte, Lorenzo L., Lorenzo's son, 104, 105, 115.
Da Ponte, Luigi, Lorenzo's brother, 2, 6, 35, 49, 78.
Da Ponte, Luigia, Lorenzo's daughter, 93, 104.
Da Ponte, Matilde, Lorenzo's daughter, 105.
Da Ponte, Nicolò, Venetian Doge, 1.
Da Ponte, Orsola Pasqua, Lorenzo's stepmother, 2, 3.
Da Ponte, Paolo, Lorenzo's half-brother, 76, 96, 99, 106.
Da Ponte, Serill, Lorenzo's great-grandson, 105 f.
Da Ponte's family, 1, 2, 52 f., 95, 96.
De Biasi, Pasquale, *Article in "Il Carroccio,"* 132 f.
Del Gallo, Marquis, 72.
De Marchi, Emilio, XV.
Dent, Edward J., XVII; *Mozart's Operas,* 60 f.
De Tipaldo, E., 5 f.
Dolfin, Daniele Andrea, 54.
Dondorologi, 20.

Don Giovanni, XI, XVII, 49 f., 63-70, 126 f., 127, 128.
Doria, Gabriello, 40, 97.
Dorigutti, 55.
Dresden, 45-49, 51, 83, 84; Opera House, 45, 49, 51.
Durant, Cornelia, Lorenzo's daughter-in-law, 105 f.
Dux, Bohemia, 33 f., 83, 84.

Eitner, Robert, XVII; *Biographisch-biobliographisches Quellen-Lexikon der Musiker und Musikgelehrten,* 56 f., 65 f., 68 f., 70 f., 90 f.
Elizabeth of Brunswick, 94.
Elizabethtown, N. J., 108, 109.
Epistola to Casti, 52 f.
Equivoci (Gli), 55 f., 64.
Evelina, 94.

Farinelli, Arturo, XVII; *Article in "Giornale storico della letteratura italiana,"* 64, 67.
Farra Soligo-Boregan, 22 f.
Farsetti, Daniele, 14.
Farsetti, Giuseppe, 14, 15 f.
Fasti Goriziani, 43.
Federici, Vincenzo, composer, 88 f., 100.
Ferdinand IV of Naples, 72.
Ferdinand, Archduke of Austria, 72.
Ferrarese, cf. Gabrielli-Del Bene.
Filemone e Bauci, 50.
Filosofo punito (Il), 65.
Finto cieco (Il), 58.
Flora e Minerva, 72.
Florence, 98.
Fodor-Mainvielle, Josephine, singer, 128.
Forcellini, Marco, 14.
Foscarini, Sebastiano, 54.
Foscolo, XII, 48, 97.
Francesconi, Daniele, 5.
Francis I of Austria, 56 f., 72, 79, 80, 129.
Francis, Dr. John W., XVI, 137, 138; *Old New York,* 47 f., 116, 117.

Frassen, Father Giuseppe, 30.
Frederick Augustus III of Saxony, 45, 47, 48.
Frottola per far ridere, 133.

Gabrielli, Bishop of Portogruaro, 7.
Gabrielli-Del Bene, Adriana, singer, 73, 75, 76 f., 80 f., 97.
Gamba, Bartolomeo, XV.
Gara degli uccelli, (La), 43.
Garcia, Manuel, 125-29.
Garcia, Manuel, Jr., 125.
Garcia, Maria, cf. Malibran.
Garcia, Signora, singer, 125.
Gassmann, F. L., composer, 49 f.
Gazzaniga, Giuseppe, composer, 58.
George IV of England, 94, 117.
German tragedy translated by D. P., 44.
Giurati, Domenico, XV; Article in "Illustrazione italiana," 99 f.
Giustiniani, Bishop of Treviso, 19, 21, 22, 30, 31.
Gluck, 53.
Goldoni, XV, 11, 15, 31 f., 56; *Le Bourru bienfaisant*, 56; *Le donne puntigliose*, 11 f.
Gorizia, 41-46; Colonia Sonziaca, 44.
Gottlieb, Frau, singer, 63.
Gould, manager of the Drury Lane Theatre, 102.
Gozzi, Carlo, 14, 15 f.
Gozzi, Gaspare, 14, 15 f., 29, 31, 32.
Grahl, John, Lorenzo's father-in-law, 78, 79, 81, 82, 84, 108.
Grahl, Nancy, cf. Da Ponte, Anna.
Grahl, Peter, Lorenzo's brother-in-law, 81, 82, 112, 113.
Granelleschi, cf. Accademia dei—.
Grant family, 112.

Gratitudine (La) o sia la difesa delle donne, 44.
Gray, Thomas, 35 f.
Grétry, André Ernest Modeste, composer, 94.
Guadagni, composer, 89 f.
Guardassoni, impresario, 69.
Guarini, Giambattista, *Il pastor fido*, 71.

Hague (The), 87, 88.
Hall family, 112.
Halleck, Fitz-Greene, XVIII, 116 f., 127, 138.
Haller, 33 f.
Harvard University, XI.
Hayden, Captain, 107.
Hillhouse's *Hadad*, 137.
Hone, Philip, Mayor of New York, 132.
Horace, 28.
Huber, Father Michael, 47-50, 84.

Isola del piacere (L'), 91.
Italia (Sull'), 116, 117.
Italian (Study of) in America, 109-12, 114, 115-17, 119-23, 129, 133-35.

Jahn, Otto, XVII.
Joseph II of Austria, 49, 50 f., 51, 53-58, 61-68, 70-72, 80, 89 f., 108, 133.

Kelly, Michael, XVII, 85, 86; *Reminiscences*, 56 f., 57, 58, 63, 64. 91.
Koch, Theodore W., XVII.
Krehbiel, Henry E., XVII, 71 f.; *Music and Manners in the Classical Period*, 92, 93 f,. 105 f., 109 f., 122 f., 127 f., 136 f., 137-39.

La Chevanne, M. C. D. de, XV.
La Harpe, J. F. de, 44 f.
Lamartine, XV; *Cours familier de Littérature*, 68.

INDEX

Landau, Markus, XVI; *La letteratura italiana alla corte d' Austria*, 57 f.
Lange, Aloysia, singer, 70.
Lantieri family, 43.
Laschi, Signora, singer, 63.
Laste, Natale dalle, 14.
Leight, Fanny, 116 f.
Leopardi, XII, 27.
Leopold II of Austria, 71-73, 75-80.
Ligne family, 87.
Ligne, Prince of, 57.
Littlefield, Walter; Article in "The New York Times," XII f., 71 f.
Livingston, John R., 118.
Löhner, E. von, XVI.
London, 36, 55 f., 74, 83-94, 98-106, 108, 125 f., 126 f., 131; Drury Lane Theatre, 85-94, 96, 98, 99, 101-5.
Lorenzi, Abbé Bartolomeo, 33.
Louis XV, 33 f.
Louis XVI, 84, 86.
Lozzi, Cesare, XV.

Macneven, Dr., 137.
Malibran, Maria Felicia Garcia, 126, 128.
Malibran, Monsieur, 126 f.
Mandini, singer, 63.
Mara, Gertrude Elizabeth Schmoelling, singer, 85, 86.
Mara, violoncellist, 86 f.
Marchesan, Angelo, XIII, XIV, XV; *Della vita e delle opere di Lorenzo Da Ponte*, 8 f., 13 f., 19 f., 21 f., 22 f., 23, 26, 32 f., 52 f., 69 f., 105 f., 137.
Marcolini, Count Camillo, 47, 84.
Maria Louise of Naples, 72.
Maria Theresa of Austria, 43, 46, 50 f.
Maria Theresa, Archduchess of Austria, 68.
Maria Theresa of Naples, 72.
Marie Antoinette, 80, 84.
Maroncelli, Piero, 137.
Martini, Vincenzo, composer, 55, 56, 64-67, 74, 90, 91, 133.
Martin y Solar, Vicente, cf. Martini.
Mathias, Thomas, 100, 120 f.
Matthews, Brander, 116 f.
Mazzolà, Caterino, 45-49, 51, 84.
McVickar, John, 110.
Méhul, 94 f.
Meissner, Alfred, XVI.
Memmo, Andrea, 31 f.
Memmo, Bernardo, 31, 33-35, 45, 75, 96 f.
Memmo, Tribuno, 31 f.
Mercadante, 131.
Merope, 90.
Metastasio, 3, 47 f., 50, 51 f., 54.
Metternich family, 87.
Mezenzio (Il), 78, 86.
Michelini, Antonio, 71 f.
Milton, 38 f., 100 f., 120 f.
Mocenigo family, 49 f.
Molmenti, Pompeo, XIII, XV, XVII; *Carteggi Casanoviani*, 31 f., 36, 47 f., 54 f., 75 f., 76 f., 77 f., 80 f., 82 f., 84, 85 f., 88 f., 91 f., 93 f.; *Venice, its Individual Growth*, 10 f., 11 f., 13 f., 15 f.,
Monico, Giuseppe, 22 f.
Monroe, President, 105 f.
Montani, Giuseppe, XV.
Monti, XII.
Montrésor, singer, 131.
Moore, Bishop Benjamin, 110.
Moore, Clement Clarke, 110, 115, 120-23, 136, 137.
Moore, Nathaniel F., 110.
Morichelli, Anna Bosello, singer, 89-91.
Moroni, *I Minuetti*, 12 f.
Mozart, Leopold, 59, 61.

INDEX

Mozart, W. A., XI, XII, XV, XVII, 52, 58, 59, 65, 66, 69, 74-76, 127, 128, 133, 140; Early operas, 60 f.; *Le nozze di Figaro*, 53 f., 59-63, 108; *Don Giovanni*, 49 f., 65-70, 126 f., 127, 128; *Cosi fan tutte*, 71, 92 f.; *Magic Flute*, 74; *Requiem Mass*, 74.
Musset, 126 f.
Napoleon, XII, 47 f., 96.
Nardini, Leonardo, 99 f., 101, 103.
New York, XII, XVI, 14, 78 f., 92, 104, 107-140; Columbia College, cf. Columbia University; General Theological Seminary, 110 f.; Opera in N. Y., 125-33; Public Library, 113; N. Y. University, 104 f.
Nicolini, Fausto, XV; *Notes to the "Memorie" in the Laterza edition*, 39, 41 f., 44 f., 54, 68 f., 69 f., 72 f., 73 f., 78 f., 79 f., 97 f., 98 f., 99 f., 101 f.
Nohl, Ludwig, XVII, 67 f.
Novati, F., XV.
Nozze di Figaro (Le), XI, 53 f., 59-64, 68, 70.

Odori (Ditirambo sopra gli), 9.
Orsini, cf. Rosemberg.
Ossian, 35 f.
Ovid, 50.

Pacini, 132.
Padua, 4, 5, 34, 35, 97; University of, 4, 35.
Paggi, Serafino, XV.
Paietta, Orsola Pasqua, 2.
Paisiello, 53, 60.
Paradisi, 85 f.
Pasta, Signora, singer, 126 f.
Pasticcio (Il), 71, 78, 130.
Pastor fido (Il), 71.
Paul V, 10 f.
Pellico, Silvio, 137.
Pendleton, E., 110.

Perceval, 100 f.
Perucchini, Girolamo, 4.
Petrarch, XI, 4, 65, 115.
Pezzana, A., 4.
Philadelphia, 105, 107, 114, 132.
Pincherle, Rachel, Lorenzo's mother, 2.
Pisani, Giorgio, 38, 44, 45.
Piticchio, Francesco, composer, 65, 72.
Pittoni, Baron, 72, 82.
Pompadour, Madame de, 33 f.
Portogruaro, Seminary of, 6-9, 12-14.
Prague, 68, 69, 83.
Prescott, 120.
Profezia di Dante (La), 119.
Provoost, Bishop, 110 f.
Psalms, 47, 48.

Raccanelli, Pierina, 4, 6.
Ratto di Proserpina (Il), 102.
Ravà, Aldo, XV; *Article in "Marzocco,"* 86 f.
Redi, 9.
Rey, composer, 94.
Ricco d'un giorno (Il), 42 f., 52-55.
Righini, Vincenzo, composer, 57, 65.
Riley, I., 109.
Riva-Finoli, 131-33.
Rohan family, 87.
Rosa, W. A., 120 f.
Rosemberg, Count Olindo Orsini di, 51, 54, 58, 62, 63.
Rossich, singer, 126.
Rossini, 126, 128, 131, 132.
Rousseau, J-J., 23, 24.

Sacchini, Anton Maria, composer, 53 f., 94.
Saggi Poetici, 9 f., 22 f., 25 f., 26 f., 27 f., 30 f., 44 f, 52 f., 101.
Salieri, 49-57, 59, 65-67, 69-72, 133.
Salisbury, Marquis of, 86 f.
Sallust, 21 f.
Salvioli, composer, 132.

INDEX

Saur, Count, 80.
Saxe-Weimar, Prince of, 118 f.
Saxony, Elector of, cf. Frederick Augustus III.
Schiedermair, Ludwig, *Die Briefe W. A. Mozarts und seiner Familie,* 59 f.
Schiso, Biagio, 14.
Schönbrunn, Court Theatre, 56.
Scott, Sir Walter, XII, 100 f.
Scuola delle amanti (La), cf. *Cosi fan tutte.*
Scuola de' maritati (La), 92.
Semira e Azor, 94.
Shakespeare, 64.
Smith family, 112.
Solleciti, cf. Accademia dei—.
Sonetti per la morte di Anna Da Ponte, 131.
Sonetto codato, 38.
Spencer, 100 f.
Stafler, G., 130.
Stanze al conte di Waldstein, 88.
Stanze al patrizio Zaguri, XIII, 2 f., 37, 41 f., 53.
Storace, Anna Selina, singer, 53, 63.
Storace, Stefano, composer, 53 f., 55, 64, 85, 86.
Storia americana, 134.
Storia della compagnia dell' opera, etc., 133.
Storia della lingua e letteratura italiana in New York, 129.
Storia incredibile ma vera, 133.
Strassoldo family, 43.
Stratico, Mgr. Giandomenico, 33.
Sunbury, Pa., 112-115.

Tasso, Torquato, 4, 66.
Taylor, William, 88-90, 93, 94, 98-102.
Teschen, Peace of, 41, 43.
Teupolo, Bartoldo, 12 f.
Tiepolo, Angela, 7, 9, 12-20, 97.
Tiepolo, Angela's brother, 18, 97.
Tiepolo, Giacomo, Venetian Doge, 12 f.
Tiepolo, Lorenzo, Venetian Doge, 12 f.
Torri, Alessandro, 129 f.
Torriani family, 43.
Trent, Council of, 1.
Trento, Giulio, 21.
Treviso, 21, 22, 95, 96, 130; Seminary of, XIV, 13, 19-32.
Tributo del core (Il), 86.
Trieste, 44 f., 74, 76-84, 130.
Trionfo dell'amor fraterno, cf. *Castore e Polluce.*
Tron, Niccolò, 14.
Tuckerman, Henry T., XVI; Article in "Putnam's Magazine," 42, 114 f., 137, 138.
Tuns family, 43.
Tuscany, Princesses of, 69.

Velez, Luis de Guevara, 64.
Venice, XVII, 1, 6, 7, 9-20, 30-40, 44, 45, 49, 51, 53, 54, 67, 75, 94, 96, 97, 129, 130; Barnabotti, 38; Caffé de' letterati, 14; Esecutori contro la bestemmia, 40; Grandi, 38; Inquisitori di **Stato,** 15; Major Council, 38; Piombi, 33 f.; Ridotto, 11, 18; Riformatori, 30-32; Senate, 31, 32.
Verplanck, Gulian C., 137.
Vienna, 37, 41 f., 45 f., 46, 47 f., 49-73, 76-80, 85 f., 86 f., 93, 97; Italian Theatre, 51-72.
Viotti, 89 f.
Vismes, des, 89 f.
Vittorio Veneto, cf. Ceneda.
Voltaire, 33 f., 34 f.
Voti (I) della nazione napoletana, 72.

Waldstein, Count Joseph Karl von, 33 f., 83, 88.
Wallack, James, 132.

Ward, Samuel, XVI; *Sketch on the Life of Lorenzo Da Ponte of Ceneda,* 47 f., 122 f., 138.
Warwick, 44 f.
Weigl, Joseph, composer, 72, 133.
Wetzlar, Baron von, 52, 59.
Wilder, Victor, *Mozart,* 68 f., 69 f.

Wilson, James Grant, XVIII; *The Life and Letters of Fitz-Greene Halleck,* 116 f., 126 f., 138 f.; *The Poetical Writings of Fitz-Greene Halleck,* 118 f.
Winter, Peter, composer, 102, 133.

Zaguri, Pietro Antonio, XIII, 2 f., 31, 33, 35, 36, 37, 40, 41 f., 53, 75, 76.
Ziborghi, Canon, 6.

COLUMBIA UNIVERSITY PRESS
Columbia University in the City of New York

The Press was incorporated June 8, 1893, to promote the publication of the results of original research. It is a private corporation, related directly to Columbia University by the provisions that its Trustees shall be officers of the University and that the President of Columbia University shall be President of the Press.

The publications of the Columbia University Press include works on Biography, History, Economics, Education, Philosophy, Linguistics, and Literature, and the following series:

- **Columbia University Contributions to Anthropology.**
- **Columbia University Biological Series.**
- **Columbia University Studies in Cancer and Allied Subjects.**
- **Columbia University Studies in Classical Philology.**
- **Columbia University Studies in Comparative Literature.**
- **Columbia University Studies in English.**
- **Columbia University Geological Series.**
- **Columbia University Germanic Studies.**
- **Columbia University Indo-Iranian Series.**
- **Columbia University Contributions to Oriental History and Philology.**
- **Columbia University Oriental Studies.**
- **Columbia University Studies in Romance Philology and Literature.**
- **Records of Civilization: Sources and Studies.**
- **Adams Lectures.** **Carpentier Lectures.**
- **Julius Beer Lectures.** **Hewitt Lectures.**
- **Blumenthal Lectures.** **Jesup Lectures.**

Catalogues will be sent free on application.

LEMCKE & BUECHNER, Agents
30-32 WEST 27th ST., NEW YORK

COLUMBIA UNIVERSITY STUDIES IN ROMANCE PHILOLOGY AND LITERATURE

EDITED BY HENRY ALFRED TODD AND RAYMOND WEEKS

FREDERIC MISTRAL, POET AND LEADER IN PROVENCE. By Charles Alfred Downer, Ph.D. 12mo, cloth, pp. x + 267. $2.00 net.

CORNEILLE AND THE SPANISH DRAMA. By J. D. Segall, Ph.D. 12mo, cloth, pp. ix + 147. $1.75 net.

DANTE AND THE ANIMAL KINGDOM. By Richard Thayer Holbrook, Ph.D. 12mo, cloth, pp. xviii + 376. Illustrated. $2.50 net.

THE INDEBTEDNESS OF CHAUCER'S TROILUS AND CRISEYDE TO GUIDO DELLE COLONNE'S HISTORIA TROJANNA. By George L. Hamilton, A.M. 12mo, cloth, pp. vi + 159. $1.50 net.

THE ANGLO-NORMAN DIALECT. A Manual of its Phonology and Morphology, with illustrative specimens of the literature. By Louis Emil Menger Ph.D. 8vo, cloth, pp. xx + 167. $1.75 net.

CORNEILLE AND RACINE IN ENGLAND. A study of the English Translations of the Corneilles and Racine, with special reference to their representation on the English stage. By Dorothea Frances Canfield, Ph.D. 12mo, cloth, pp. xiii + 295. $2.00 net.

THE VERSIFICATION OF THE CUADERNA VIA, as found in Berceo's Vida de Santo Domingo de Silos. By Josn Driscoll Fitz-Gerald, Ph.D. 8vo, pp. xiii + 112. Facsimiles. Paper, $1.25 net; cloth, $1.50 net.

PIERRE LE TOURNEUR. By Mary Gertrude Cushing, Ph.D. 12mo, cloth, pp. xi + 317. $2.00 net.

THE DEVELOPMENT OF STAGE DECORATION IN FRANCE IN THE MIDDLE AGES. By Donald Clive Stuart, Ph.D. 12mo, cloth, pp. ix + 230. $1.75 net.

CHARLES DE SAINTE-MARTHE. By Caroline Ruutz-Rees, Ph.D. 12mo, cloth, pp. xvi + 664. $2.25 net.

THE SYMBOLISM OF VOLTAIRE'S NOVELS, with special reference to Zadig. By William Raleigh Price, Ph.D. 12mo, cloth, pp. vi + 269. $1.75 net.

PARTICIPIAL SUBSTANTIVES OF THE -ATA TYPE IN THE ROMANCE LANGUAGES, with special reference to French. By Luther Herbert Alexander, Ph.D. 8vo, pp. xii + 163. Paper, $1.50 net; cloth, $1.75 net.

UNCLE AND NEPHEW IN THE OLD FRENCH CHANSONS DE GESTE. A Study in the Survival of Matriarchy. By William Oliver Farnsworth, Ph.D. 8vo, cloth, pp. xii + 267. $2.00 net.

COLUMBIA UNIVERSITY PRESS
LEMCKE & BUECHNER, Agents

30-32 East 20th Street   New York

COLUMBIA UNIVERSITY STUDIES IN ROMANCE PHILOLOGY AND LITERATURE

Edited by Henry Alfred Todd and Raymond Weeks

DIDEROT AS A DISCIPLE OF ENGLISH THOUGHT. By R. Loyalty Cru, Ph.D. 12mo, cloth, pp. xiii + 498. $2.25 *net*.

LI ROMANS DOU LIS. By Frederick C. Ostrander, Ph. D. In Memoriam. 8vo, cloth, pp. vii + 154. $1.75 *net*.

EUROPEAN CHARACTERS IN FRENCH DRAMA OF THE EIGHTEENTH CENTURY. By Harry Kurz, Ph.D. 8vo, cloth, pp. xii + 329. $1.75 *net*.

THE USE OF THE INFINITIVE INSTEAD OF A FINITE VERB IN FRENCH. By Benjamin F. Luker, Ph.D. 12mo, cloth. $1.50 *net*.

THE GLORIA D'AMOR OF FRA ROCABERTI. Edited by H. C. Heaton, Ph.D. 8vo, cloth, pp. xiii + 167. $1.75 *net*.

FRENCH CRITICISM OF AMERICAN LITERATURE BEFORE 1850. By Harold Elmer Mantz, Ph.D. 12mo, cloth, pp. ix + 165. $1.75 *net*.

THE SPIRIT OF PROTEST IN OLD FRENCH LITERATURE. By Mary M. Wood, Ph.D. 8vo, cloth, pp. xii + 201. $1.75 *net*.

THE INFLUENCE OF ITALY ON THE LITERARY CAREER OF ALPHONSE DE LAMARTINE. By Agide Pirazzini, Ph.D. 12mo, cloth, pp. xii + 168. $1.75 *net*.

TIRANT LO BLANCH. A Study of its Authorship, Principal Sources and Historical Setting. By Joseph A. Vaeth, Ph.D. 8vo, cloth, pp. xvi + 169. $2.00 *net*.

FRENCH TERMINOLOGIES IN THE MAKING. By Harvey J. Swann, Ph.D. 8vo, cloth, pp. xxii + 250. $2.25 *net*.

THE EXTRAORDINARY VOYAGE IN FRENCH LITERATURE BEFORE 1700. By Geoffroy Atkinson, Ph.D. 8vo, cloth, pp. xiii + 189. $2.00 *net*.

INFINITIVE CONSTRUCTIONS IN OLD SPANISH. By Wilfred A. Beardsley, Ph.D. 8vo, cloth, pp. xiv + 279. $2.50 *net*.

MODERN PROVENCAL PHONOLOGY AND MORPHOLOGY. Studied in the Language of Frédéric Mistral. By Harry E. Ford, Ph.D. 8vo, paper, pp. v + 92. $1.50 *net*.

TOULOUSE IN THE RENAISSANCE. Part I. By John Charles Dawson, Ph.D. 8vo, paper, pp. xiv + 87. $1.50 *net*.

LORENZO DA PONTE, POET AND ADVENTURER. By Joseph L. Russo, Ph.D. 8vo, cloth, pp. xviii + 166. Illustrated. $2.50 *net*.

COLUMBIA UNIVERSITY PRESS

Lemcke & Buechner, Agents

30-32 East 20th Street   New York